The 5L's

Live, Love, Laugh, Let go, and Let God!

Donquies Sledge

ARCHWAY
PUBLISHING

Archway Publishing books may be ordered through booksellers or by contacting:

Archway Publishing
1663 Liberty Drive
Bloomington, IN 47403
www.archwaypublishing.com
844-669-3957

ISBN: 978-1-6657-3334-2 (sc)
ISBN: 978-1-6657-3333-5 (hc)
ISBN: 978-1-6657-3335-9 (e)

Library of Congress Control Number: 2022921100

Print information available on the last page.

Archway Publishing rev. date: 12/06/2022

INTRODUCTION

The five Ls are all about life. They are about having a better way of life. The five Ls are all about how to become a better person. This book will address families, friends, relationships, kids, and everyday life routines.

I'm not perfect. No one's perfect. The life that you lead can go a lot easier if you live it with positivity. In everyday life there's a lot of negativity out there. It's hard to stay positive in a world of negativity. I have learned that, by applying the five Ls, anything is possible. What you get out of life is all about what you put into it.

It's not easy out here in the world trying to live positively when you see a lot of negative influences. There is a lot of temptation out there. Temptation is everywhere you look. It's all about how you live your life and how you interact with others.

I try to see the good in everyone. If we all see the good in each other, maybe, just maybe, this world would be a better place.

Look at your life now and ask yourself this question: Am I really happy?

I found myself asking that question a lot. No, I wasn't happy. Who am I? That's another question I asked myself, and I didn't know the answer to that one either. I decided I would have to look within myself and change who I was in order to find my happiness.

Now I know who I am. I am me! Sometimes, you must look

within yourself to find who you are. I used the five Ls to learn who I am.

Here they are—the five Ls:

1. Live
2. Love
3. Laugh
4. Let go
5. Let God

These are the five simplest concepts to live by. In this book, I will explain what those words mean. They represent five easy ways to turn your life around. I know it's hard in this world of negativity, but it is possible to be positive.

You have to *live* your life to the fullest. *Love* is not impossible to find. *Laughter* is a way to find peace within yourself and share it with others. *Let go* of all the hate, anger, and the negativity that's in your soul and heart. *Let God* handle your problems. Always put him first.

Now I'm about to break each one of these concepts down and explain how each one of them has worked in my life. They have put me on a positive level. Everyone has good in them. You just have to find a way to let it out. This book is for everyone who wants to put a little positivity in his or her life. This book is for people who want to be motivated and inspired to be great. No one is perfect. We all make mistakes. Every time I made a mistake in life, my grandfather would tell me, "You breathing, ain't you?" That means everyone makes mistakes, and if you're still breathing, you have a chance to fix those mistakes. Even though we make mistakes, we still can be great. That's what this book is about.

I'm not a psychologist. Some might say I don't have the credentials for writing this book. My qualification for writing this book is life. Life has taught that me I don't have to be perfect. Life has taught me to keep breathing and be great. It has inspired me to love myself and love others. Some people can't see how great they are. This book will guide you to find your greatness.

CHAPTER 1

Live

Are you living, or are you surviving? That's a question you need to ask yourself. Living and surviving are two different things. If you're surviving, you're just living within the confines of what you need. If you are living, you are doing what you want, when you want, and how you want. When you are surviving, you are just barely getting by. There is no shame in that. There are a lot of people who are just surviving. Where do you see yourself in five years? Do you see yourself living, or do you see yourself surviving?

I know it's hard out here in this world. You work, work, work and hope that someone is going to throw you a bone. You hope that one day your work will pay off. Sometimes you work so much that you forget how to live. Then it's hard to get out of that stage of life when your mind is stuck on the mentality of surviving. It seems as if every time you take one step forward you take four steps back. You want to get ahead in life, but every time you get to where you have some breathing room, something takes that breath away. Then you start complaining about your lifestyle. It's up to you to change it.

What you don't realize is that it's you who is holding you

back. You want a better life, but then you start thinking that you can't achieve it. Well, you're wrong! Never self-talk yourself into negativity. So many of us are unaware of how we always talk negatively about ourselves. We should not do that. We have to stay positive in our thinking. You can do anything you set your mind to. Everyone starts out at the bottom. I have to admit that some people don't start *all the way* at the bottom, but they do start at the bottom.

To start living your life, you have to take one step at a time. They say you've got to crawl before you walk, but sometimes you have to scoot yourself around on your stomach before you can crawl. That's life! You just have to play the hand you're dealt.

Life is all about how you live it. You can live life, or you can survive life. If you're not happy with your life, then get up and do something about it. If you feel that you're fat, lose weight. If you're with someone you don't want to be with, just leave. If you're unhappy with your job, get another one. If you feel that you want to go out and buy yourself something, do it. If you feel that you need a vacation, then go. You are the only one who's holding you back. You are in control of your life. You can change it anytime you want to. It's your life. Live it to the fullest. Living life means doing what you *want* to do. Not what you *need* to do.

God didn't put all these wonderful things on this earth so you could sit back and not take advantage of them. No! You need to start living. Get out and enjoy all these wonderful things that you have never done or never seen. Start living!

How many times have you said that you wanted to do something, and you didn't do it? How many times have you said that you wanted to go somewhere, and you didn't go?

How many times have you looked at your neighbors, friends, or family members going on vacations or taking trips to places that you wanted to go? You want to do it so badly but you don't. How many times has that happened to you?

Think about it! You are at work, and your boss says, "I'm about to take a two-week vacation to Jamaica." What would be your first thought? Some of you might think, *Man! My boss makes all the money. My boss is lucky. I wish I could be like that!* Others might sarcastically say "It must be nice!" Then, when someone says you could do the same thing, you come up with excuses—you can't afford it or you don't have time. Stop with the excuses! I'm telling you now that you can just throw all those thoughts out the window. Your boss did what he had to do to get in that position so he could live life.

Some people even put down Steve Harvey for becoming a success. He is an American television personality, actor, comedian, and producer. He did what he had to do to get where he is today; he sacrificed blood, sweat, and tears. Now he is living life. You can do the same.

Do what you have to do to get to where you want to be. It's all up to you! Some people say you've got to fake it until you make it. No! That's stupid! Don't pretend to be something you're not. Just be you. Why would you want to try to live like Steve Harvey on a Walmart cashier's salary? That doesn't make any sense. You have to be you until you make it. You don't have to fake who you are. Just be you.

Another thing! Don't try to be like someone else. There is already a Steve Harvey. There is already a Bill Gates. Again, just be you!

There are plenty of things that you can do on your budget to enjoy life—things that you can afford to do. You don't have to be rich. Get out, enjoy life, and just be yourself. You're the only person stopping you. Why don't you just get up and do it? Most of us get comfortable with our lives and complain because we are afraid of change. If there is something that you do not like in your life or something that you find yourself complaining about all the time, don't get comfortable with it. Don't be afraid to change your life for the better.

You don't want to look back on your life and say *shoulda*, *coulda*, or *woulda*. All you gotta do is do it or change what you don't like. How many times have you said to yourself, "I should have done that"? How many times have you said to yourself, "I could have done it this way"? How many times have you said to yourself, "I would have been living like this if I had done this"? How many times? Again, *shoulda*, *coulda*, *woulda*.

You're the only one who is stopping your happiness. Live life with no regrets. I'm not saying you can afford to go to Jamaica right now. I'm not saying you should buy yourself a thousand-dollar piece of jewelry. Don't spend all your money on things you can't afford. I'm not saying that. Start out small.

Say you are sitting at home with an extra few dollars in your pocket. Treat yourself to dinner and a movie. There's nothing wrong with that. Go to a ball game. Buy yourself something nice that you will enjoy. It doesn't have to be jewelry or a four-hundred-dollar pair of shoes. It can be a coffee maker or anything that you will enjoy. Some of you may think that this sounds funny, but some people actually enjoy small things like coffee makers.

If you want to go on a vacation, put a few dollars aside when you can. It doesn't have to be hundreds of dollars. It could be five or ten dollars or just change you let accumulate in a jar. Those extra quarters, dimes, nickels, and pennies add up. You would be amazed how much change you can save up. Do anything that will help you do what you want to do or get you to where you want to be—anything to get you on that vacation that you always dreamed of.

You say you don't have money like that. Well, you don't have to. There is always something you can do to start living your life. You don't even have to spend any money. Take a walk in the park or take a walk on the beach. You can even take a walk through your downtown area. No matter what you do, just live life. Get out and see the world for what it's worth.

People are always trying to tell you what to do. Some of what they say is good advice. Some of it is bad advice. Some of it is just pure garbage! Just be you. You know what it takes in this world to be successful. Just believe in yourself and listen to your heart. I used to wish I had done certain things in my life. Now I'm living my life with no regrets, and I'm hoping you live yours the same way.

When I was eighteen, I had a chance at a great life. All I had to do was finish high school and then go to college. I chose otherwise. I dropped out. I thought I was going to be the greatest music producer in the world. My music was good. People even said my music was great. I didn't think I needed to go to school. I was on the top of my game. That was the type of lifestyle I was living. I didn't think I needed a backup plan. I was it! What I failed to realize was that what goes up must come down. People started turning their backs on me—the people I thought were going to be there. People took what I produced for them and left. Everyone started being out for themselves. Then the music switched up. The music didn't sound the same anymore. I got fed up with it all. I gave it all up. I should have had a backup plan. I could have been successful a long time ago. It would have been great if I had had that backup plan. *Shoulda, coulda, woulda.*

It's never too late to try again. It doesn't take a lot. Just do something for fun at least one day a week. Some people enjoy just working around the house. Some people like to go into the park and feed birds. No matter what it is, make sure you enjoy it because that is what living life is all about.

Most importantly, enjoying life is being who you are. Don't let anyone come into your life and tell you who you are and what you like. You know what you like, and you know who you are. If you like bowling, and someone tells you to go play pool, but you don't like pool, how are you going to enjoy yourself? Even if someone says "Let's go out to the club tonight" and all you like to do is watch TV at home, how are you going to enjoy yourself doing things you don't like to do? Make sure to choose to do what you enjoy. Make sure it's something that you want to do. Just because you like fishing, that doesn't mean the next person likes fishing.

Peer pressure is something else. This sort of pressure drives you to do things you don't want to do. My advice to you is don't fall into the trap. Love yourself more than you love doing things you don't want to do. Love yourself enough to say you want just as much out of life as you put into life.

When I was a teenager, my brothers didn't want to hang out with me, but it was OK. They had their own lives. The thing that got to me was that, every time they went out to play basketball or just hang out, they never bothered to call me and ask if I wanted to go. They hung out with everyone but me. Then I got older. I was about twenty. My brother finally asked me to go out with them. I didn't want to go. At this point of my life, I was more of a homebody. I stayed home so much that I didn't want to go anywhere. My brother kept at me until I finally said I would go. I went out with him. That was a mistake.

We went to a club. I had never been to a club, but my brother has been there multiple times. He knew the rules; I didn't. I was wearing a windbreaker outfit. Before we left the house, he should have told me all the club rules and how to dress. When I got to the door of the club, the bouncer told me that I couldn't enter because I was wearing running pants. Now let me remind you: my brother asked me to go out with him, so I rode with him to the club. He saw what I had on before we went to the club.

We were at the door. The bouncer turned me around. My brother looked at me, shrugged his shoulders, and said he was not taking me back home to change. He went into the club. I had to sit outside the club for hours. There were people fighting outside the club. There were people shooting outside the club. Now I was dodging bullets, ducking down behind the car. A couple of guys came up to me. One of the guys said that I had been in the club looking at his girl, and they wanted to fight me. The girl told them it wasn't me; it was another guy. I had to sit out there all night until my brother got ready to go. That wasn't a good night for me.

The point is, I wasn't even there because I wanted to be. I was there because I had let myself be pressured into going. Don't let peer pressure get to you. Be you! Do what you like to do.

Do you really want to work all your life just to pay bills? If you work all week long, why can't you enjoy some of your earnings? When you get a day off, do something that you want to do—whatever you like to do. Think of it as self-love. I'm not telling you to go out there and be selfish. What I am telling you is to love yourself. There is a big difference between self-love and being selfish. Self-love is loving yourself and doing better in life. You teach yourself how to love so you can love others the right way. Selfish is thinking only about yourself, and that can lead you to self-destruction. There's nothing wrong with loving yourself. It helps to build your self-esteem and motivates you to be better in life. It also helps you to love others. How can you love others if you don't love yourself? Well, you can't!

Living is a way of life that you have to feel within yourself. It all starts with you. Are you tired of the same routine? You go to work, and then you come home. You repeat this over and over. What living do you actually do? That's not living. Well, a little about me. I used to work for the county in the parks and recreation department. I used to cut grass. All I ever did was go to work and go home. As soon as I got home from work, I'd take a shower, eat my dinner, and go to bed. That was the same routine day after day.

On my days off, all I wanted to do was just go back to work to try to make more money so I could pay the bills. If I couldn't find extra work, then I would just sit around the house and do nothing. I was just surviving day after day, week after week, month after month, and year after year. I had to find myself. I had to look deep within myself to find myself. So I asked myself, was I living or surviving? I was only surviving. I was going to work just to pay bills. That's not a way of life.

I heard some family members talking about going on cruises. I heard friends and coworkers talk about their long vacations to beautiful places. They talked about how beautiful everything was and how vacationing was so much fun. All I did was sit around and hear all about their vacations. I wanted a piece of the action. I thought to myself, *So how do I do it?* There is always a way. I just had to look within myself to see that.

I learned that I didn't have to have any money to actually go out and explore. I just simply walked through my downtown area. I noticed a lot of different things that I had not noticed before. I wondered what other things that I hadn't noticed. Then I started putting money aside—not a whole lot of money because I wasn't making a whole lot of money. I just put five or ten dollars aside when I could so I could do things. In a short amount of time, I had saved up some money—enough so I could go explore different places. I had to start small. You can do the same thing.

Write out a list of things that you want to do. Write out a list of things that you want to see. Start out with the easiest and least expensive things you want to do, and do those first. For the more extravagant things, just save up by putting a bit of money aside when you can. Hold on to that money and don't touch it. You will be able to do it. I'm telling you—I believe you can do it. It's not only me who has to believe that you can do it. You have to believe that you can do it.

Again! I don't make a whole lot of money. I'm not a rich man. I have a nine-to-five job just like most people, but my goal for the year is to spend Christmas in New York. With my income, I know that I have to save up. That's one of my goals for the year. That may not sound like much to some people, but that is a goal that I set for myself. That is something that I can afford.

Yes, I want to go to Egypt. I can't afford it right now, but that is a long-term goal that I set for myself. And I will accomplish it. Set yourself a goal. Start out with a weekly goal. That's a short-term goal. Think of something that you want to accomplish every week. It doesn't have to be huge. Just something simple—something that you know you can do. Next, set yourself a monthly goal. This should be something a little harder, but something you can afford. Then set yourself a six-month goal. You might have to save up for this one. Then you set yourself a yearly goal, something you want to do at least one time in your life. Now that you're on a roll, set up three-year and five-year goals.

No matter what your goals are, never give up on them. Your yearly goal might be going fishing for two days in another county. Or it might not be as big as going to France for the summer, but that's okay. That could be a long-term goal that you set for yourself, but you have to be determined to reach that goal.

As I said before, your first goal doesn't have to be extravagant.

It could be as small as visiting another city that is nearby. It could be anything.

Another way of living is to follow your dreams. What are your dreams? What are your goals? When I was a little kid, I either wanted to be a weatherman, a singer, an actor, an author, a football player, a football coach, a wrestler, a radio host, or the governor of Florida. No! I did not achieve any of that. I ended up losing my way.

As I grew up, I lost all my childhood dreams. I thought my life would go one way, but it took a turn and headed the other way. I had to discover who I was. Now I have found myself. I know who I am. Do you know who you are? What are your childhood dreams? Are you fulfilling your childhood dreams?

You are only as successful as you feel you are. You should never lose your hopes or your dreams. You should always hold on to them. That is what helps you live. Now, let me be honest. We may never fulfill all our childhood dreams, but some of us will. My two biggest dreams are becoming governor of Florida and being a football coach. Will that happen? I don't know, but I'm not going to give up.

Being shut down from achieving some of our dreams shouldn't stop us from being successful. Always remember that one dream opens another dream. I might not be a wrestler, a weatherman, a singer, an actor, a football player, a football coach, or the governor of Florida, but now I'm writing this book! I will be successful. You can be successful too. It's all in you to decide if you're going to be successful or not.

What are your dreams? If you never fulfilled your dreams, would you think of yourself as successful? You can still be successful even if you do not fulfil your dreams. You have the ability to be as successful as you want to be. You have the power.

There is a lot of negativity out there. If we listen to it, we can convince ourselves that we can't be successful. Well, I'm telling you that you can. Look deep within your heart. Look deep within your soul. You will see that you're a better person than anyone says you are. You just have to believe in yourself. You just have to believe in your goals. You just have to believe in your dreams. You can be successful. Don't let anyone tell you that you can't. Once you start believing the negative influences in your life, you have already lost. I'm here to tell you that you don't have to lose. Just be who you are.

Say you want to go to Japan but you can't go this year because of your finances. Yes, that is a downer, but you can still achieve that goal. So what if you can't go to Japan this year? If you want to go someday, put your mind to it. You can go to Japan next year. This year, go to the library and do some research on the places you want to visit in Japan. Learn a few Japanese words. I'm not telling you to do something that I'm not doing myself.

I'm just a poor country boy who didn't have anything. Now I am on my way to my success. When I was growing up, my family was very poor. We often didn't have food to eat. We didn't have running water. But we had each other. My life started out with a whole lot of nothing, but I had a whole lot of dreams and hopes. As I got older and became a teenager, I started feeling that no one had my back, so I started letting go of my dreams. I started letting go of my hopes. I'm telling you now, you don't have to do that!

Make living your best life a part of who you are! People are going to say that you can't do what you want to do. People are going to shut you down the moment you try to go after your dream. People are going to tell you that you are a fool for trying. That should be the fuel to the fire. Nothing should stop you. Their negative comments should be your motivation to be the best person you can be. Don't let anyone or anything stop you.

Why should you be unhappy because others are unhappy? Unhappy people don't care about your life. Unhappy people want to make everyone else unhappy so they can feel better about their lives. They only care about what's going on in their lives. Unhappy people are selfish people. Since they're unhappy, they want to keep you unhappy. You should never let a toxic person into your life. Toxic people will bring you down so that you will have nothing. Toxic people are very negative; they have nothing good to say about anything or anyone. Those are the things to watch out for. Live your life, and always put God first.

I remember riding in the truck with my former boss one day. We were discussing politics and talking about how our town was being run. We started talking about the crime rate. I told him what I would do if I was sheriff, and I jokingly told him I should run for the office of sheriff of Escambia County Florida. My boss got serious. He told me that would never happen; I would never become sheriff. That made me so mad. That put fuel to the fire and motivated me to think about what I would have do to get there. I started planning to go to school for political science. Then I thought about it. Do I really want to become sheriff? No! That was not one of my childhood dreams. That was not really what I wanted to do. That was a joke that had escalated. I didn't want to become something that I really didn't want to be just because someone's negativity pushed me in that direction. It had all started out as a joke. It's not living if you are doing something that you don't want to do.

A part of living is doing something that you love to do rather than something you have to do in order to survive. Don't let someone push you out of your comfort zone. Don't let someone push you into doing something you don't want to do. Do I like the job that I have now? No! Am I living? No. Am I surviving? Yes! That's all I will ever do if I don't change my path. I'm telling you now that I'm changing it, and you can too.

Who wants to just go to work, come home, take a shower, eat, go to bed, and do the same routine every single day? I don't know about you, but I don't. I want more out of life, and I'm going to get more out of life. This is coming from a dirt-poor country boy who had a zero chance of becoming successful. I made a way. I made my chance grow from zero to a hundred percent, because I believed in myself. I invested in myself. You need to start believing in yourself.

There have been plenty of times when I wanted to give up, but I kept pushing. I kept breathing. I never gave up. Life will test you just to see how passionately you want what you want. You have to want it a lot. I played high school football. When we had a game, I used to look up in the stands and see all the people. There were hundreds of people. All of my teammates had family sitting up there, but no one had come to the game to root for me. There wasn't anyone there for me. After the game, my teammates' family members and friends congratulated them when we won and consoled them when we lost. I felt so empty inside because no one had come to see me. That made me feel like no one cared about me, so I gave up the game.

What I'm saying is this: I shouldn't have given the game up. I should have kept pushing. I should have kept going. There's no telling how far I could have gone. Sometimes you will stand alone. Sometimes it is going to be harder than you expect. You should never give up. Always be your best no matter what you do. I have walked away from a few opportunities in my life. Yes! I do regret it. Now I'm here to change my life and make sure I correct those mistakes.

Standing alone is not a curse. Sometimes it's a blessing. God will show you that you can do anything alone. He shows you that you don't need anyone else but you. Take heed and listen because the only thing you need is you.

As a kid, on some holidays, I stood alone. One Christmas I went into the woods and chopped down a tree. When I got home, I looked throughout the yard and found little items that would serve as gifts. I scrounged around for any kind of paper, and I wrapped those little items I had found. I pretended they were gifts. I didn't have tape, so I used rope and string to secure the paper.

On Christmas morning, we had a tree! It wasn't a real Christmas tree, but it was a tree, and I had put gifts under it. These were not gifts that people had given me; they were just things I'd found in the yard. I woke up and opened the gifts on Christmas morning. This may not sound like a wonderful Christmas to you, but it was a wonderful Christmas to me. I never gave up hope on that Christmas.

On one Fourth of July, I was all alone. I didn't eat anything that day. I pretended that my family was there, and we were having a big family BBQ. We had a few acres of land surrounded by woods. People lived in big houses on the other side of those woods, and they were shooting fireworks up high in the air. I sat there and watched those gorgeous fireworks, pretending that it was my family members who were shooting them off.

I was alone on Easter. We couldn't afford a lawnmower, so the grass was kind of tall. I wanted an egg hunt! Because I didn't have eggs, I found little rocks and other small treasures, and I pretended they were eggs. I had fun hiding them all around the yard.

Another year on Thanksgiving I sat alone. I thought to myself, *Why don't I just start my Christmas gathering early?* So again, I went to the woods and cut down a tree. I put it up on Thanksgiving. Back then, I thought it was beautiful. That Thanksgiving, I started a tradition, and now on every Thanksgiving, I put up my Christmas tree.

As a kid, I never lost faith, but as I got older, in my teen years, I started losing my faith. Now that I'm grown and look back at myself, I realize that, as a kid, I was so blessed. I was never alone because I always had God. I am telling you—don't lose faith. Anything is possible.

I look at where I started and where I am at now. Miracles happen every day. All I'm saying is this: Life is not easy, but you have to keep your faith. You have to keep your hopes. You have to keep your dreams. You have to keep breathing. You have to keep pushing. It's all up to you. You have to live your life. No one else is going to do it for you.

As a kid, I was living. I just didn't know what it meant to

live. Now I do. As a teenager, I started surviving. As a young adult, I continued surviving. Now that I am an older man, I am wiser. I know what it takes to live, and I know what it takes to survive. I'm telling you now, you have to know what it takes to live and what it takes to survive, even if you have to go back to your inner child. Find a way to live your life. I can tell you from experience that *living* is a lot better than *surviving*.

There is nothing that should ever stop you from living. You should always live. Stop all that surviving. Surviving causes depression. Surviving causes anger. Surviving causes envy. You look over at your next-door neighbors, and you see them with things that you want. It's not hard to achieve those things. Like my grandfather said, if you can believe it, you can achieve it.

All you have to do is do it. Get up, go out, and do it. Some people are happy with their lives. If you're happy with your life, I'm happy for you. Keep doing what you're doing to stay happy because that's what's important is you being happy.

I wasn't happy with my life. That's why I decided to change it. If you're not happy with your life, you need to change it.

I started going back to school a few years back, and I met a guy who had just got out of prison. He didn't want the life he had before he went to prison; he wanted to change it. He was going back to school so he could do better in life. He changed his life for the better. He went back to school to learn heating, ventilation, and air conditioning (HVAC). Now he's making good money, and he doesn't have to worry about anything. He is living his life. He is doing what he wants to do. He is now living his childhood dream. Don't tell me it's not possible, because it is. This guy spent ten years in prison. He got out of prison, went to school, got a job, and is now living his dream. Don't say it can't be done because he did it.

People with felony records always say. "I've got a record. No one will hire me." Get that out of your head. I have seen people do what others call impossible. The only person that is stopping you is you. Your success or lack of success has nothing to do with a felony. It has nothing to do with your record. You can get out and do what you want to do. Stop blaming your lack of success on your past mistakes. All of that doesn't matter. You are the only thing that matters.

If you blame your lack of success on your record, you are just using an excuse and you really don't want to change and live your life the way you want to. You didn't want to do that in the first place. Don't blame your lack of success on anybody else. Blame it on yourself. People who want to get out and do something will do it regardless of any drawbacks they might use as excuses.

I have a nephew who has a felony. Now he is a boxer, and he owns his own lawn care business. He got out of prison and wanted to make a change. He took it upon himself to make a better life. He did it because he wanted to. You can't tell me it can't be done. Yes, it can!

Some people out there are holding down two jobs just to survive. That is not a way of living. That is the way of surviving. You don't have to have two jobs and only survive. You can do whatever you want to do. You just need to figure out a way to do something better in life. All you have to do is know what you want to do and do it.

If you work all day at a fast-food restaurant and also work all night at Walmart, you don't have time to live. That is not living. That is just surviving. You work hard, and all your money goes to bills. No! You should never do that unless that's something you really want to do. I'm not knocking it. That's something you might enjoy doing. And, if that's something you want to do, you are living.

Find something you enjoy doing and get paid well for doing it. Let's just say you want to be an electrician. First you have to study up and learn what's needed to become an electrician. You might need to attend classes. If that's the case, you have to find the right school and sign up for the right classes. Once you become a certified electrician, you will have to find a job that is right for you. Make sure that it's the job you love and are comfortable doing. That way you won't spend all your life at a job or jobs that you do not like. I am living testimony. I spent five years at one job that I didn't like. Then I spent five more years at another job I didn't like. I do not want to survive any longer. I want to live. I want to do things that I want to do but still do things that I have to do. No matter what, bills have to be paid, and the family still has to be taken care of. I'm not saying give up your life for something you want to do. You have to do what you have to do first. Then you can do what you want to do. You have to do things to get your life going. You have to survive to live.

In life, you want to live a little. You want to have fun. There are plenty of wonderful and beautiful things on this earth to see and do. You go to work, come home, eat, take a shower, and go to sleep. You end up missing out on all the wonderful things that life has to offer. Answer me this: Do you really want happiness, and are you willing to make the necessary sacrifices to get it? When I say sacrifices, I mean making some cutbacks to save money or doing what you have to do to start your career. Most of you will say you want happiness, but when it comes to the sacrifice part, some of you will back out or come up with excuses of why you can't do it. No more excuses. It's all on you to make your life better.

Most of you can find happiness if you only change one thing in your life. Only you will know what must be changed so you can achieve that happiness. It could be your relationships, your friends, your family members, your weight, your job, or just your daily routine. It's up to you to take hold of your happiness. Deep down you know what you have to do to find your happiness. Now I'm going to say this again: surviving is what you have to do to live. Living is what you want to do. Are you living or surviving?

CHAPTER 2

Love

To me, love is one of the most important Ls. Love is family members, friends, husband, wife, children, God, and most importantly you. Love is not impossible to find. Love is already in you. Some people just don't know it. Love is the most powerful emotion there is. Love conquers all. Love can make you do the impossible. Love will make you do something that you never thought you would be able to do. You will do things that you never did before.

Let me be honest. Love can be your greatest ally or your worst enemy. Let me explain! Love is a two-way street. If one of those streets is broken or cracked up with potholes, get ready for a bumpy ride. Sometimes, if you go down that street, you find that it's a dead end. You try so hard to find an alternate route, but no streets seem to be the answer, so you try to go off road, but you are not built for off road. So what do you do? You try to help build the road. You try to do everything you can to build that road perfectly. But, because you don't know how to build a road, the road you work so hard to build ends up lumpy, bumpy, and full of holes.

People even try to help other people build their roads, but

you can't build a road for another person. We all have to build or own road. Additionally, if a person doesn't want to build a road, there's nothing you can do besides get out of the way. Call on God to ask him for his guidance because, if you keep going, your car is either going to break up or run out of gas, or you're gonna eventually come upon an ocean you cannot cross. Be careful and make sure your love is not a one-way street. You will end up traveling alone.

Sometimes love hurts. All you can do is be yourself and love people the best way you can. You also must know when to let go. It is important to understand when people are ready to be loved.

Some people don't know how to be loved or don't know how to receive love. Maybe they have been dogged out all their lives, and by the time they find the right person, they are broken. They are not bad people. They just don't know how to love or accept love. Knowing how to give love and receive love the right way is very important. Giving love is in our nature. That's automatic. Now, some people find it difficult to receive love. When someone is showing love, it's important to know when and how to receive it.

Feeling lonely when you are in a relationship is not good. If you tell your partner how you feel, if that person really loves you, he or she will do anything possible to make you feel less lonely. Always remember, however: You can't change people! People have to change themselves! If your partner throws your feelings to the side and does not try to at least talk about your feelings, then he or she might not care for you the way you care.

A relationship must be fifty-fifty. Someone who cares for you will listen and do whatever necessary to address your feelings. Maybe your partner doesn't talk to you enough. Maybe your partner doesn't hold you enough. Maybe your partner doesn't go anywhere with you. Maybe your partner isn't at home enough. Maybe, if your partner is at home, he or she is doing everything possible to avoid you. If your partner truly loves you, he or she will do whatever must be done to make you not feel loved rather than lonely.

Talk to your partner about how you feel. Communication goes a long way. Partners should be willing to listen and do something to help each other feel more comfortable in the relationship. Be willing to do what it takes to be with your partner. If your partner ignores you or blows an issue off as if it's nothing, then it's time to let that person go.

How do I describe the perfect relationship? Easy! There isn't one. Love, faith, trust, and loyalty—that's what a relationship needs. There are three elements that make a relationship work: the mental element, the spiritual element, and the physical element. Let's break them down.

The Mental Element

Your partner is your friend. You laugh and cry together. Your partner is there emotionally for you no matter what you go through. He or she is always there for you. Good or bad. That is your best friend. You should be able to talk to your partner about anything. He or she has your back through thick and thin and will put you first through it all. Your partner loves you unconditionally and is not quick to give up on you or the love that the both of you built together. Your partner is equal to you in your relationship and shares the truth about everything, whether it's good, or bad. He or she won't judge you or your past and doesn't disrespect or degrade you. Your partner just loves you for who you are and is your strength in life.

The Spiritual Element

Your partner is there to keep God in your life, to be there for you, and to keep you on the right path by giving good advice and the right guidance that you need. He or she motivates you to do better in life. Your partner never puts you in harm's way and serves as your protector. He or she connects with your soul, helps you feel good about yourself by giving you compliments no matter if you're having a good day or a bad day. He or she makes you believe that you will succeed and you will feel good about yourself. Your partner lets you know how much you are loved every day and makes you feel loved every day. Your partner makes your soul feel at peace.

The Physical Element

Your partner looks good to you in his or her own way. No matter what others may say, your partner has to be the best-looking person in the world to you. Sex isn't the most important aspect of a relationship, but sex should make you feel so amazing, as if there is no one else who can make you feel the same way. Your partner makes you feel like you're the most beautiful or handsome person in the world. Your partner can please your mind, heart, body, and soul.

You need all three of these for love to work. *Two out of the three will not work!* Always remember that, if things start fading, always start back at the beginning. Go back to what made both of you fall in love in the first place. That is the way to last. People fall in and out of love every day. Falling in love is easy. Maintaining that same love requires a lot of work, and some people don't want to put forth the effort to keep that love from falling.

When you are in love with someone, that person has to be the most beautiful person in the world to you. You and your partner have to have love, trust, respect, and honesty. You must be loyal and understanding, and you must communicate well. I will come back to those words later on.

You should always keep passion in the relationship. Again! Let each other know how you feel. Tell your partner that you love him or her every day. Give him compliments. Tell her how sexy she looks, especially if she is having a bad day. Let your partner know how important he is to you, and to the world. Make each other feel special, as if there is no one else on the planet but you two.

People lose sight of that as the relationship grows. My thing is, you have to go back to whatever got you two together in the first place. Again! Start back at one. Love can be the most wonderful thing. It takes a real man and a real woman to maintain a lasting relationship. No relationship is perfect. You will have ups and downs. You will have disagreements.

Give each other space and time to miss each other. Do not be under each other's feet all the time. When you two come together after work or otherwise spending a day apart, you should feel as if you are seeing each other for the first time. Every time you look into each other's eyes, you should feel as if you are falling in love all over again. It should be like that every time. I'm not saying that being in a relationship is easy, but true love does conquers all.

Now there are other key ingredients in a relationship. We've talked about the mental, spiritual, and physical aspects. In order to keep a car engine running smoothly, you have to tune it up occasionally. And a relationship requires the same maintenance care. That is where the next three elements come in: compromise, sacrifice, and patience. These are essential for us to achieve love, trust, honesty, loyalty, respect, understanding, and communication.

The Element of Compromise

Compromise! Now remember those words I said earlier? You have to compromise with each other. You have to have respect. You have to have understanding. Understanding two people coming to an agreement. It is not one saying something and the other agreeing just to make the other one happy. Both of you have to come up with a solution, and both of you have to have respect the decision that you make together. Both of you have to stay true to that decision. If you make a decision together, one of you can't decide to dishonor it. No! Respect the decision both of you made.

Let's say that she doesn't feel like cooking tonight, but you want a home-cooked meal. The two of you will have to work it out. He has to think, *She has been cooking all week long. Maybe it's time for her to have a break from the household chores. Everyone needs a break every once in a while.* That shows respect and understanding and leads to compromise.

Respect and understanding go a long way in a relationship. They show that you can respect each other's minds and understand what each of you is feeling about a situation.

Compromise affects all areas of a relationship—things we may consider small or big. It could be as small as choosing whether to buy white or wheat bread, or as big as choosing where to go on vacation.

Let's say you both want to go on vacation. One of you wants to go to Hawaii; the other one wants to go to Jamaica. You have to work it out and meet in the middle. Maybe you could choose to go on a cruise to the Bahamas. That's compromising.

As everyone knows, the people who come into your life can be lessons or blessings. Well, I was once in a relationship that taught me about compromising. When I first got with her, things were fine for the first month. Then things started to change. Our decisions started turning into her decisions. Every time I made a suggestion, she made a suggestion. There was nothing wrong with that. It went wrong because she didn't respect my suggestions. She never tried to understand where I was coming from. It was do it her way, or we break up, or she would fuss at me for hours.

I couldn't ever meet her in the middle on anything. It was always her way. Our breakup was over something stupid. I had to go to work all week, so I needed gas in the car. All I needed to do was make it to the end of the week until I got paid. All we had was $20. We were together in the car when I pulled up at the gas pump. She asked what I was doing, and I told her we were all most on empty, and I had to go to work all the next week. She said she was thirsty and hungry; she wanted me to spend my last $20 on a meal in a restaurant. I offered to cook when we get home. I told her I really needed the gas for work, but she said she wanted something to eat immediately. I thought about it. If I put $15 worth of gas in the car, I could probably make it to work until Friday when I got paid. I could get gas as soon as I could cash my check. I said to myself that could work.

So I suggested that she could use the $5 I would have left over to buy something to snack on, like some chips or something, and a soda until I could get home and cook for her. But she said no! She wanted to go across the street to a restaurant. She said that what she wanted cost $15, and she told me I could put $5 worth of gas in the tank, drive to work on Monday, and then catch the bus or carpool for the rest of the week until payday.

I asked her how she expected me to catch the bus with no money or carpool without sharing the gas costs. I told her that all the bills were paid, and we had lots of food at home. Anything she wanted to eat, we had it. I told her she didn't have to do anything; I would cook for her.

She started getting loud and started calling out my name and throwing things out the window. It got so bad, I had to drive away from the store. We went home. When I parked in the driveway, she demanded the keys to the car. I gave them to her, and she drove off. I thought she had just left to go cool off, so I went into the house and cooked a nice supper. I waited for her to come back, but she never did until midnight. At that point, I knew I had to go to work in the morning, and if I said anything to her, she was going to argue, so I didn't say anything.

The next morning while she was sleeping, I got up, got dressed, and went to work. When I came home, all of my stuff was strewn about the yard, and she was gone. She had written a letter and taped it to the front door. It said that she wanted me gone before she got back. She had changed the locks and everything. She had kicked me out and then gone to meet a guy who had just got out of prison. That relationship was a big lesson on compromising. She wanted her way or no way.

The Element of Sacrifice

Sacrifice shows how much you really care for your partner. It shows that you are willing to give up a part of yourself and your goals in order to have a better life with the one you love. Always remember to sacrifice only to make the relationship better.

Let's say that you always wanted a boat. You have just saved up enough money to buy it, but your woman's car breaks down. The money that you saved is just enough money to get her car running. You know she needs that car, but you have been saving up for a boat for year. What do you do? That shouldn't be a question. If you love that woman, you sacrifice what you want for what she needs. It is important to sacrifice in a relationship.

Now, here's another scenario. Ladies, you have a job, it is payday, and you have just received a nice bonus. You have been wanting a special diamond ring from your favorite jewelry store, but you remember that your man just sacrificed his boat for what you needed. What do you do? That shouldn't be a question either. If you truly love someone, sacrificing for your relationship should not be a question.

If someone you love sacrifices what he or she loves for you, that shows how much you are loved. You need to show your partner how much you love him or her. You have to show your love. That's called sacrificing for the one you love.

I was in one relationship with a woman who did not sacrifice anything. I loved her with everything I had—my heart and soul. When we first got together, everything seemed fine. She told me things that had been going on in her life. She told me how people had been mistreating her. She told me how men had disrespected her, especially her own father, who had never done anything for her. She had low self-esteem. She said she desperately needed a car. She had kids that she needed to take care of. I understood that. So what did I do? I got her a car.

As time went on, we moved in together. I move to another state to be with her. I sacrificed everything I had built up for her when I moved. I helped build her confidence up. She really was a beautiful girl with low self-esteem. Over time, her confidence built up higher than I had expected. One day we were sitting on the couch watching a movie. She looked over at me and said that she wanted to become a stripper. I had a problem with it at first, so we talked. Then I said okay. I was trying to compromise. Big mistake!

She started going out. She started going out a lot. That left me to take care of her kids. I spent a great deal of time with them, treating them as if they were my own. I believe that, if your with someone who had children, those children are your responsibility too. With that being said, every morning I got up and got them ready for daycare and school. When they got out of daycare and school, I picked them up.

Back then, I had my own recording studio. Between making sure the kids were okay and working in the studio, I never really had time to myself. I was doing it. It was all good. She really didn't have to do anything. On the weekends, my kids would come to our house, and her kids would go off with their dad. One day while my kids were there, some of my clients wanted to work in my studio for a few hours. I asked my partner what she was doing that afternoon, and said nothing. I asked her if she could watch my kids for a few hours while I was in the studio, but she said no; she had to go get her nails done. Every time I asked her to help me out, she refused. She sacrificed nothing!

My car wouldn't start one day. I asked her if I could borrow hers. Well, by that time, she had made enough money to buy a better car than the one I had given her. My mom needed me to go to her house and fix a broken water pipe; she had no running water. Let me remind you that my mom lived in another state about forty-five minutes away. That's not that far, but it's a fair distance. My partner didn't want to lend me her car at first, but then she said okay. I didn't know that she agreed because she wanted to spend time with another guy.

As soon as I got to my mom's house, my partner called and said she needed her car so she could go get her hair done. I didn't even get a chance to fix the pipe. On the way home, I thought about how much I loved my partner and how much I had sacrificed to be with her. I decided to try to talk to her when I got back, but she already had it in her mind to break up with me. That crushed me to my soul. When I asked her why she was leaving me, she said that I didn't make enough money.

The lesson I learned from that is, if you really, truly love someone, there is nothing wrong with sacrificing for that person. That shows that person how much you care.

The Element of Patience

Patience is something we all need, but it can really strengthen a relationship. Patience shows that you are willing to go through anything to be with your partner. Once you have that bond, it will be impossible to break. Let's say your partner has a demanding boss who expects her to spend extra time at work. That doesn't mean she doesn't want you or doesn't want to spend time with you. It doesn't mean she is putting other things before you. She is just doing what she needs to do to live. Responsibilities come first; you must be responsible and maintain the lifestyle you live. Have patience with the one you love, and it will all work out in the end.

If you have patience, you have loyalty. Loyalty is something that is hard to come by. If your partner tells you that he has to work late, you probably don't like it. You want him to be home as soon as possible, but you wait. You are showing him that you are putting your trust in him to be home when he said he would be. Loyalty and trust are not easy to find. Most people nowadays are looking out for themselves.

I was dating a woman who became my fiancée. Again, as it had been with my other relationships, it was good in the beginning. We were always together everywhere; we did everything together. I started a new job. Every time I came home, she would be mad. I always wondered why. She was mad because she wasn't getting enough time with me.

We would always argue and fuss. It got so bad we broke up for a month. I started going back to school. We ended up getting back together. Then she had a problem with me going to school. She said I was only going to school to see other women. To keep the peace, I had to drop out of school. That was a big mistake. That was something that I didn't want to do.

As time went on, I ended up going back to my old job. She started complaining again about me not giving her enough time, but I did not have the time for her that she wanted, so it was back to arguing and fussing. As time went on, we started drifting apart. She started going out and doing things, leaving me alone at home. She ended up finding someone else. I guess she thought he would spend time with her. We broke up—again. She didn't have enough patience for me to go to work eight hours a day, five days a week. She thought that I was out doing other things when I was just working so I could feed the family.

You have to have patience. You have to have trust. You have to have loyalty. To be in a relationship, those three have to go together. Patience plays a big part in a relationship. Men, sometimes your lady doesn't want to be intimate. That doesn't mean she is out there cheating. That doesn't mean she is out there doing something she isn't supposed to do. Sometimes women just aren't in the mood. Have patience with her. Let her know that you love her. Let her feel that you love her. Everything will work out for the best. Having a strong woman on your side is better than having a weak woman who is pretending to be.

Communication in Compromise, Sacrifice, and Patience

Communication plays a big part in compromise, sacrifice, and patience. It is very important to always communicate clearly and honestly with your partner. If there is something that you feel a certain way about, don't hold it in. Holding it in just makes the situation worse when you finally let it come out.

Communicate with your partner and say how you feel. If your partner loves you as much as he or she promises, he or she should be willing to listen to what you have to say, and do possible to correct any problem you might have. If you are with someone who sticks with you through all your problems and insecurities, you are with a person who is willing to do what it takes to keep you. Keep God first, and your bond will be even stronger.

Never confuse lust with love. Lust is something you can get off a street corner. Lust is just sexual feelings. When you're done, there is nothing left to hold onto. The other person soon leaves, or if he or she does stay, it's only for a second round of sex. I'm just telling it like it is. If you get on the phone, and all you talk about is what you're going to do to each other sexually, and you never talk about your future together, that is just lust. Love is everything. The right love will make both of your souls feel as one. Love will make you a husband or wife.

Now I love sex—don't get me wrong. But it has to be with someone I love. It's best if it's with the person I want to spend the rest of my life with. Then sex is the best feeling in the world. Some people don't get it. That's where lust gets confused with love. Then they start cheating on the person who truly loves them.

Today, some people think it's okay to cheat. It's not okay. You hear people bragging about having something on the side. That's not right at all. I can't understand it! When did it become okay to have or to be a side piece? Why would you want to go through that drama instead of having a peaceful heart? Call me old fashioned, but I am a family man. It only takes one for me. One is enough. I can barely keep up with one woman; why would I make it two or more? That would make me go insane. No! But seriously, one is enough, people. Why would you want to hurt the one you love? You just make it harder for the next person to come in and love that person the right way if you two don't stay together. You should always love your partner the way he or she should be loved. If you're not feeling love for that person, you should let him or her go instead of causing pain. If you're causing pain, you don't love him or her as much as you say you do.

News flash—love is not supposed to hurt. It's supposed to make you feel on top of the world. Do the right thing. Love the right way or let your partner go to someone who wants to love him or her the right way. People always look at what's on the outside of a person, or they worry about what people think. Lots of times, you miss your blessings when you worry about what others think.

You might be with a person who is a little bit overweight or not that cute, but to you he or she is handsome or beautiful. That person might be the best person you've ever been with. That person just might be your blessing. If people start saying bad things about that person, and you think of breaking up because you're worried about being talked about, you might just be missing a blessing that God sent to you.

God always sends you what you need in your life, but if you keep asking God for what you want, he will take away what you need. Be careful what you ask for! God is going to give you what you want to show you that's not what you really wanted. You'll soon figure it out. What you wanted is what God sent you the first time because that was what you *really* needed.

Never be ungrateful. You can throw your blessings away if you don't look at the inside of a person's heart. Don't ever treat people in an ugly way because that will make you the ugly one. Love is not to be seen. You can only feel love. Love comes from the heart and soul. You can only lust with your eyes. Sometimes your eyes trick your heart into thinking you love someone when you are just feeling lust.

What is true love? True love starts with friendship, not sex! Your lover should always be your best friend—someone you can count on for anything. I can't stress that enough. I'm going to say it again. Your lover should be your best friend. You and your lover should always be as one. You should know each other's minds, hearts, bodies, and souls. Love should not be based on looks. Love should be based on what's in your hearts. You should always have an understanding with your lover. When you look deep within that person, you should see his or her pain, struggle, laughter, joy, and daily ups and downs. You should be there for your partner through it all. When you start doing that, you get to know that person truly and intimately. That's a friendship.

If you don't have friendship in a relationship, you don't have anything. The number-one thing that keeps friendships close is God. You have to always keep him first over it all. Your lover should be your life partner. Always keep in mind. It has to go both ways; it will not work if only one person is trying.

Men, pay attention! Sometimes you could be with a woman who has built a protective wall around herself because she has been hurt a lot. If you care for her, and if you are a real man, you will figure out how to get around that wall or go over it or through it for the woman you love. Also, you have to remember that she has to want it as well. You have to treat her right and love her. Remember, if she smiles at you, that doesn't mean she is happy, so you have to be there for her no matter what. She is not going to let you know everything from the start, and there is nothing wrong with that. She is just trying to protect her heart, and as men we have to respect that.

Sometimes she just needs a shoulder. Be that friend she needs. You have to be her best friend—someone she can run to for anything. When you have her full love, she will love you like no other. A woman's love is the greatest gift she can give you. She will be the best thing that ever happens to you. Just be there for her and comfort her in her time of need.

Also, men, your woman's menstrual cycle can cause her to go through a lot of emotions. That is definitely not a time to argue. If you really care for your lady, you will stick by her side no matter what she is going through. We, as men, don't know how it feels to have cramps and mood swings. We, as men, should be understanding of our queens. If we really care for our loves, we will have patience with them. You have to understand she is hurting, bloated, and doesn't want to be aggrieved. You have to make her feel loved and wanted. I know it's hard because she can get mean. We need to be there for them like they are there for us when we mess up and do dumb stuff. Men, let's get it together and be real men, not just for ourselves, but for the ones we love.

Women, pay attention! A man should provide for, protect, and love his queen. If he is doing everything he is supposed to do to keep you happy, you should have his back through it all. The key to a man's love is that a woman has to be loyal, and she has to have his back through thick and thin.

Think about it! Have you ever seen a man and a woman together, and you think to yourself, *I don't see why he is with her. She is no good for him.* Well, I'm going to tell you this: He feels that women will stand with him no matter what. He feels that she is the one he can trust because of her loyalty. A man who respects a woman opens doors or brings home flowers because it's Tuesday. He tells her how sexy she is even when she gets sick or is feeling down. He motivates her for success. He spends time with her. He stays loyal and faithful. He goes to war for her. He protects her and provides for her. He never calls out her name. He makes love to her like none other. All she has to do in return is give him her loyalty and her happiness.

Now don't get me wrong! There may be some women who don't want to be treated that way, but most women do. If a woman has a good man and she sees him working in the yard, there is nothing wrong with taking him something cold to drink and telling him how much he is appreciated. Men need to hear that from time to time. Let him know and make him feel as if he is the only one for you.

Men and women! Be who you are. Never lower your standards for anyone, and the right one will come along. Love can feel good. Love can also hurt, but in God's hands everything will be okay. Always keep God first. You have to stick by each other and have each other's backs. Don't let anyone come between you.

You can only go as far as your partner will allow you to. If you want to be a doctor, and your partner is always putting you down, always telling you how you're not going to make it, that partner really doesn't care about you or your future. Your partner probably doesn't care where he or she is going in life either. Both of you have to work together to achieve your goals.

Let me explain it like this: Imagine your relationship is like a motorboat. Now imagine that you are that boat. Your partner is the engine of the boat. The engine moves fast. That engine moves constantly. That engine keeps you going. The engine does not keep you in one spot your whole life. That engine is what motivates the boat to keep going and going. You will not stop with a great engine pushing you.

Now let's say you're a rowing boat. Your partner is the oar. Your partner is rowing you along. Now you're moving slowly and you are not motivated very much, but still you are somewhat motivated. You're not reaching your goals in a timely fashion. It takes you longer to reach your goals, but the most important thing is you're still moving.

Now let's just say you are a sailboat. You are the boat and your partner is the sail. If something is happening that your partner likes, the sail goes up, and the boat gets moving—not as fast as the motorboat, but it's moving at a good pace. But as soon as a storm comes, the sail goes down. So now the boat is sitting until the conditions improve. When something goes wrong, the sail doesn't want to weather through the storm. The boat will move only when it wants to move or when it serves a good purpose.

Now let's just say you're a boat with no motor, no oars, and no sail, or no. Now you're a boat that's not really moving anywhere. This means your partner is not holding you back, but he or she is not helping you move forward either. You may succeed in life, but it's going to take you longer because you have a partner who is not helping you. That partner is there just for the ride, content with life as it is. That partner really doesn't care if you make it or not. You're just drifting along slowly by yourself. You're not getting any motivation out of your partner. You're not getting anything; you're just at a constant drift.

Now let's say your partner is an anchor. Now you are not moving. You're not going anywhere. You're stuck in one place. That partner is hurting you. Every time you try to move, your partner tries to throw some negativity at you. You will not succeed in life with a partner like that. Sometimes you have to cut the anchor off and just drift. Be careful who you end up with. Everybody is not a motor. I have been with a few anchors in my life. I had to learn the hard way and cut them loose.

Letting go of someone is difficult, especially if you are in love with that person. But letting go of a person who is not good for you will turn out to be the best thing for you. I'm not going to lie—it's going to hurt. Depending on how deep your love is, it's going to take a while to get over the separation, but once you do, you will see a brighter future. As time goes on, you will feel better about yourself. You will build your self-esteem. You will start motivating yourself. Then you will start accomplishing your goals. You will start to feel like your old self. One day you will look back at the person you were with, and you will laugh and say, "I don't know what the hell I was thinking!"

Take your time to find that special someone. You know what you're worth. You know what you like. You know what you love. Take your time for that special someone. There's no reason to rush on anything. I know getting with someone could be tricky at first. You need to go slow and find out who that person really is. Look at that person and see how he or she treats other people. That's how that person is all the time. If that person treats other people as if they're no good, you will receive the same treatment. If that person is constantly arguing and fussing with other people, he or she is going to argue and fuss with you. If that person is always negative towards everything, he or she will be negative toward you. If that person treats people well and is doing good things in life, he or she will treat you well and help you in life. You have to know what you're worth. No one else can tell you that. Don't get out there and start a serious relationship with someone you don't know. That can end up disastrous for you.

Some people share a relationship with their soulmates in the friendship zone. When you ask that person, "Why won't you date that friend?" They will come up with something like, "I don't want to mess that friendship up." God will send you a person just for you, but you will not date that person because of how that person looks, or you might not date him or her because of what your friends might think. You might not date that person because of the way that person dresses. You might not date that person for whatever the case may be. Now your soulmate is stuck in the friend zone with you. You don't want that person, so God sends your soulmate to another soulmate. Your soulmate is now happy with someone else. You might end up with someone who is appealing to you but who treats you badly. You might end up throwing away your blessing in exchange for someone who is no good for you all because you were listening to your flesh and not your heart. I really can say that has happened to me.

It is important to learn to recognize your blessings. If you do, you will get everything you want in a relationship. It will turn out to be the best thing for you. Some of you pray for what you want, but when God sends it to you, you act as if you don't want it. When he sends you what you asked for, you'd better be ready for it. People blame God for relationships that go bad. It's not God's fault that you messed up and missed out on your blessing. It's your fault! Be with someone who makes you happy. Be with someone who makes you laugh and smile. Be with someone who makes you feel good about everything. Be with someone who is positive. Be with someone who motivates you. Be with someone who makes it easy for you to love him or her. Be with someone you are compatible with. Be with someone who is going to hold you up through thick and thin. When you find that person, you will have to humble yourself. Do the right thing and compromise with him or her; make the necessary sacrifices. Have patience, but he or she must do the same for you. If that person is not willing to try, let the relationship go! You will be a better person without it.

Sometimes what you think is meant to be for you is actually meant for someone else. Sometimes two people can be good people but not good together. You have to learn what is for you, and what is not for you. You just have to learn to let go.

Never approach your relationship the way you approach a job. Let's be honest. Do you really want to work at a backbreaking job every until you are dead, every day wishing for another job while your boss gets on your nerves? In a relationship, your partner can get on your nerves. Sometimes you call into work and say you can't come into work that day. In a relationship you might say you're hanging with the boys or girls that day. On a job, I take time to go on vacation. In a relationship, I take time to go to the club with the boys or girls, and I stay gone all night. Spend time with your partner. Go out with your partner, and have fun together. Never make your relationship like it is a job because you will always have an excuse about something. Always remember to have fun. Your partner is your best friend, and your best friend is your partner. Never let anything or anyone come between that.

Lots of relationships come to an end over money. True love outshines money any day. I see plenty of homeless couples. That is the real meaning of true love. Money only lasts until it is spent. True love lasts a lifetime.

What I am trying to say is this: money isn't everything. True love is. If someone is after you because of what you have, that is not the person for you. When you first meet someone, give the relationship time to grow. Let the other person see who you are and spend time finding out who the other person is. The one who looks at who you are rather than at what you have and what you look like will be the one you need. Real love is not hard to find, but real love is hard to maintain. Again, always start back at the beginning when things get out of hand.

Laugh

How many days out of the year have you been happy? How many days out of the year have you been sad? How many days out of the year have you been angry? If you're angry, and sad days outweigh your happy days, that's not a good thing. Laughter is good for the heart and soul. Some people even say laughter leads to healing. I agree! Laughter is something we all need. Laughter is the key to happiness. Think of a time when you were angry or sad and someone came to you and made you laugh. After that laughter, how did you feel? For a brief moment, you found happiness. Those troubles briefly left your mind. That laugh relieved some of your stress level, and we all know that, in some form or fashion, stress kills.

My life got so messed up one time that the ups and downs sent my stress levels went through the roof. I am a person who loves to laugh, and I enjoy making people smile and laugh. For a whole month, things kept coming at me in a negative way. I went through a bad breakup. I felt that my son had turned his back on me. I felt that everyone I tried to talk to about my situation was pushing me away. It seemed to me that no one wanted to have anything to do with me. I felt all alone; I had no one to talk to. I was left all alone with multiple circumstances weighing heavily on my mind. It got so bad, I stopped eating and stopped hydrating. One day at work, I started feeling sick. I felt as if I was going to pass out. I got dizzy and had to lie down for a while. When I felt a little better and figured it would be safe for me to drive, I made my way to my car and drove myself to the hospital. The doctors ran all kinds of tests. The results indicated that my stress was killing me. I was messed up! I was constantly by myself, and I had been spending a lot of time thinking about my troubles and all the negativity I was going through. I shouldn't have been alone. I should have gone out somewhere to keep my mind from getting bogged down in negativity.

When you are sad and hurt, you don't want to interact with the public. You want to stay cooped up in a room somewhere all alone. That's not good! The best thing you can do is get out and interact with positive people. That is what I started doing. I decided to go fishing one morning. I saw a group of older men at the lake. They were laughing and having themselves a good time. I didn't think anything of it. The next morning, I went back down there and encountered the same group of men, still laughing and having a good time. I still didn't think anything of it. When I went there on the third day, one of the older men walked up to me and started talking. We ended up having a nice conversation. He got into his life story and told me all about what he had gone through and how he had started drinking. He told me he used to drink all the time, but the drinking just caused him more problems. Finally, he had given up drinking. Soon he started cracking jokes, and he made me laugh. For that one moment, I didn't feel pain. I didn't feel sad. I didn't feel hurt. I felt good. I felt happy. It had been so long since I felt happy. I started interacting with the other guys. We laughed and fished and had a good time.

Force yourself to get out of the house and interact with people. You never know who God has placed in your life to make you laugh. At that time, I was in a relationship. She was angry every day. I tried bringing her flowers; she still was mad. I tried buying her things like jewelry. That did work; she stayed angry. No matter what I did for her, she stayed angry. She fussed a lot. She yelled a lot. There was nothing anyone could do to make her happy. She was just a human full of negativity. That was beginning to stress me out. I just had to let go of her to better myself. I could not afford to allow her to stress me out. I had to stay away from the negativity.

Sometimes you have to move away from negativity. Try to keep your life positive. Let go of the negative friends. Hang around positive friends. You will see that your whole attitude improves. You will feel better physically. You will even feel better mentally. Not everyone will be positive; there is a whole lot of negativity in this world. There's nothing we can do about that, but we can do something to make ourselves feel happier. Positivity is what we all need in our lives. How many times has hearing a child's laughter made you feel happiness deep within? Children are innocent. All they know is what you teach them in life. Some parents try to be their children's friends. Big mistake! Kids need parents first, friends second. You can be your children's friend, but be their parent first. They will have plenty of so-called friends who will come and go in their lives.

They need a parent more than anything. They need someone to teach them right from wrong and someone who will provide for them and protect them. They need someone who will give them the right advice and lead them the right way. Always be a parent first and friend second. Children don't ask to be here. Why should we treat them like trash? Why should we treat them like slaves? Come on, people, let's stop doing this to our kids. Not all parents do this. Let's raise our kids right. We should be their parents. Not anything less. How do you raise children? I don't know everything, but I do know this—you don't have to be perfect. You just have to raise your children with love. Some people do see their kids as an income. Well, here's a news flash: they are not! They are not a paycheck. They are not there so you can get a man or a woman. They are not there so you will have a place to live. They are not there to be slaves. They are there to be your children. They are there so you can teach them right from wrong. They are there for love.

Think about this: if you get sick, who is the first one to respond? Who is the one who is constantly asking if you are all right? Who is the one who tries to make you feel better? Who is the one who is right there to have your back no matter what should anything negative go down. Tara is my daughter. She is my heart. She is my happiness. She is my princess. She is the breath that I breathe. I would be willing go to war with Satan for my daughter. I am so proud of her. I was there for everything in her life—her first step, her first day in school. When she was a kid, I used to do her hair ever morning before school. She had my heart from the top to the bottom. She was Daddy's little girl. I loved her more than anything on this planet. She had all my love. I thought there wasn't enough of love in me to share with anyone else. I was wrong. My son, Donquies the third, was born. The love I had grew more than you can imagine. I had my boy. I would be willing to destroy everything if something should happen to him. He is my world. He is my backbone. He is my heart. He is my happiness. He is me. When my son was born, I thought I was the luckiest man in the world. He wasn't anything like his dad. He looked a bit like me, but he was a good-looking version of me. He was my handsome boy. I felt there was no greater love than the love I felt. I was wrong. As time went on, day after day, I loved him more and more. He was a better version of me. He was smart. He was handsome. He was an all-around good kid. I was working on my car one day. He was no more than three years old. He came out and helped me work on the car. I was putting a new engine, and I had to get up under the car, so I sent him in the house because I felt it would be too dangerous for him if he decided to crawl under the car with me. As he was walking off, he had the greatest smile I had ever seen. Pure joy took over me. I will never forget that feeling. I looked over at him as he was walking up the stairs, and tears started running down my face. I don't know what it was, but my love, which I thought had reached its limit, had excelled to limits I thought were impossible to reach. At that moment, my love grew more than I can ever explain. It was the most awesome feeling I ever had.

One Christmas, I couldn't do much for my daughter and son. Everything that could have gone wrong that year had gone wrong. I had to explain to my kids that they might not have a Christmas. I cried that year because I knew I had done everything right so they would have a nice holiday. They came to me one afternoon when I was particularly sad. They told me that it was going to be okay. As long as they had me, they had everything they needed. I guess that was all I needed to hear. Somehow, that motivated me to say, "Yes! They will have a Christmas." I can't even start to explain how I ended up with a sideline job to make extra money for Christmas. All I know is that I called my dad to ask him for help. I asked if there was any work that was coming up. He said there was; in fact, he had just been about to call me. A man needed some work done before Christmas because his family was going to celebrate at his house. My dad and I did the work the next day, and I made the money I needed for my kids' Christmas. That was a great Christmas. I loved watching the smiles on their faces as they opened their gifts. You have to be willing to do anything and everything to keep that smile on your kids' faces, especially when they are good kids. Children are a God's blessing.

Everyone complains about the violence in the world. The key to change is the children. We need to break the bad cycles and encourage our children with God, love, honor, good morals, and respect. How are our kids going to respect us if we don't respect ourselves? How are kids going to respect us if we keep beating on women? How are kids going to respect us if we dress half naked and post photos on social media so everyone can see them? Parents dress their kids like thugs, pimps, and prostitutes and act like it's nothing. Then when the kids start dressing or acting in a certain way that is disrespectful, the parents get mad at them. The parents did that to them.

Babies are born innocent. What we teach them is on us.

When the kids start acting out, we should try to find the reason for their behavior. It's easy to blame television, pop music, video games, and other influences in the environment they're living in. No! It's all about how and what you are teaching them. Kids are not born one way or another; they become what they are taught.

We need to stop saying, "Not my child. My child wouldn't do that." No! You don't know what your child would and would not do. Stop pretending your children are always innocent. Look into the situation first before you defend them blindly. Look into the problem and find out what role your child played in that situation. That way you can handle the problem accordingly. That is what being a parent is all about. Now you will know what your child is capable of.

When I was a child, I went to the next-door neighbor's house to play with my childhood friend. He talked me into climbing a tree with him and the other kids. I knew right from wrong. We weren't supposed to climb trees back then. My mom always told me that, if I climbed a tree and fell, she was going to whip my butt. I thought to myself, *If I climb a tree and fall out, I will be too hurt to worry about a whipping.* I knew I wasn't supposed to be in the tree with my friends, but I climbed up anyway. The next thing I knew, my friend's aunt came home and caught us in the tree. She tore my butt up. Then she called my grandfather. When I went home, he tore my butt up some more. Then he told my dad, and my dad tore my butt up. Then my dad told my mom, and she tore my butt up. I'm not telling anyone to whip their kids. The moral of the story is don't put anything past your kids, because you really don't know what they're capable of doing.

When you get in a relationship with a person who has kids, you have to show respect. Some people get together and forget about the kids. No! No! No! The kids are the most important part of any family. When you are in a relationship with someone who has kids, you should love the kids just as if they were your own. All of you should be as one—a family! I will say this again: kids didn't ask to be here. So why mistreat them? If you are going through a tough time in your relationship— arguing or whatever the case may be—the kids shouldn't ever be brought into the conflict. Kids should never be brought into grownup people's situations. Kids are God's little miracles, so why mistreat a blessing?

Kids are God's gift! Love and cherish them like nothing else, and always keep God as the head of the family. Let God lead the way and guide the family. The family will always be blessed. Family is very important. Your family members should be your best and closest friends. Your true real friends should be like family.

My family. What can I say? I love them all. We have our ups and downs, but we are family. I want to challenge all the people who are reading this book to contact your family members! Call them! Text them! Hug them! Kiss them! Tell you love them! You never know when will be the last time you can be with them. God calls people home every day. I have lost five people who were dear to me. My grandfather, Charlie Underwood, was the best. He always joked and laughed. He was always happy. He was the most hard-working man I have ever seen.

He worked from sunup to sundown. He made sure that the family was always running well. He put his all into the family. He didn't hate anyone. He loved everyone. He saw the good in everybody. He was a wonderful man. He loved God more than anything. He always stayed positive no matter what. Everyone loved him.

My father, Daniel Sledge, was a great man. His heart was as big as the universe, and it was a heart of gold. He would have done anything for anybody. He was always happy. He always delivered the funniest comeback jokes. He always kept a smile on the faces of those around him even when they were down.

My sister, Sheila Watson (née Sledge), was one of the most respectable people on this planet. She was a beautiful woman. She was a hard worker. She always kept her word. She loved to laugh. She also stayed happy. If people wanted something and she had it, it was theirs.

My sister, Sharon Smith (née Sledge), was amazing. She also had a very big heart. She loved to have fun. She exemplified the real meaning of living. She kept everyone smiling. If there was any way she could help, she would do it. She was the best. She lived life to the fullest.

My son, Donquies Sledge the second, was only three months old when he passed. He made me feel like I was the luckiest man on the planet when he was born.

All I am saying is that you must love and cherish the people you call family. You may never get that chance again. People are always looking for blessings, but you already have blessings. They are your family. If God wanted you here by yourself, he would have put you here by yourself. Let's stop getting together just on birthdays and holidays. Go out and do family things. My family members have been playing softball together on the weekends just so we can hang out with each other. We gather together—my kids, my mom, my brothers and sister and their kids, my cousins, and my aunts and uncles. Even close friends of the family join in. That's what family does.

We didn't have much when we were growing up. In the county where I grew up, we worked every day. We were a poor family. We worked for other people around the area. We put up fences, we baled hay, and we took care of other people's animals. We did a lot of different things. The kids (there were ten of us) had to walk to school in the heat, rain, sleet, or snow. In the summer, it got so hot when we walked home from school, I wanted to take off my shoes and shirt, but the sun was too hot on my skin, and the sand on the dirt road was too hot to walk on barefoot. In the winter, it got so cold I couldn't feel my hands or feet no matter how many layers of clothes I put on. I couldn't get warm.

We used to walk home from school, change our clothes, and go to work. After work, we'd come home and do what we had to do around the house. In the summer, we had to make sure the grass was cut. We didn't have a mower at the time. We had to use a sling blade. The yard and house had to be cleaned all year round. In the wintertime, we had to chop wood for the wood heater.

Some people may look at my childhood as growing up hard. No, it wasn't. I look at it as growing up with good morals, loyalty, trust, honor, love, and respect. We were all we had, but that was all we needed. My grandfather used to sit next to the wood heater and tell us stories of his life. At night when everything was done, I used to wrestle around with my brothers. Well, they used to beat me up. As the youngest of ten, I'll just say it that way. The girls used to put puzzles together and hang together. We had an old outside cooking pot. We sometimes lit a fire around it at night, and we would sit in the warmth, talking, laughing, joking, and playing. I had an amazing family.

As my siblings got older, they moved out one by one until I was eventually all alone. I miss those days. Now we all have our own families. We have our own traditions. Family members should always show love for one another and be there for the other family members. You should never do family wrong. Families need to have a strong bond—an unbreakable bond that will keep your family together. They should never part. Sometimes I look back at all the things I have been through and all the things I have seen. I would not change a single thing.

Real and true friends should be considered family members. People call themselves your friends. Are they really and truly your friends? Your friends should always offer that shoulder you need. They should be people you can lean on when you need help. Do you have a true friend? Are you a true friend to others? True friends are rare. If you have a real true friend, you have a blessing.

There are a lot of fake friends out there. Sometimes they are hard to spot, but sometimes it is obvious. The obvious fakes usually only come around when they need something from you. Real friends will always be around. Fake friends will give you advice you *want* to hear. Real friends will give you advice you *need* to hear. Fake friends are always sneaking behind your back talking about you. Real friends don't have anything bad to say about you and won't tell any of your business to anyone. Fake friends will perpetuate your drama and always get you into fights. You might end up in jail, lose your kids if you have any, or end up hurt. Real friends will keep you out of drama and fights and let you know when situations are not worth losing everything over. Fake friends are quick to turn their backs and leave you standing alone in a bad situation. Real friends never leave your side. Fake friends will deny you. Real friends will never deny you; they will always consider you part of their families. Fake friends will always have something to do so they can't help you when you need them. Real friends will be there for you when you need them. They might not always be able to be there physically, but they will do whatever they can to help you until they can get to you. Real friends will love you from their hearts and souls.

Throughout my elementary schooldays, I was always pushed away. I never had a friend when I was in elementary school. I never knew what it was to have a true friend until I got to middle school. Before I went to the sixth grade, I thought I was going to be "the man." I thought I was going to be "it." I was wrong. When I first got to middle school, I was treated badly; it was just like elementary school all over again. Kids picked on me. Guys didn't chose me to be on their team. I got voted out of everything. I pretty much gave up trying to be friends with people.

As soon as I adopted that mind frame and decided to give up on the friend thing, I met a goofy, nerdy kid who was just like me. He was tall and uncoordinated, but he was cool. His name is Joe. He and I started hanging out. We became the best of friends. When people saw me, they saw him. When they saw him, they saw me. We were inseparable. He invited me to his house one day. I went and met his mom and dad. They were the nicest people I had ever met. After a while, they called me their son. They loved me as if I was their own. I loved them as if they were my parents. I will never forget them. I will never deny them. They are my family. Joe and I became more than friends; he became my brother. I can truly say he is a great friend.

Real friendship has no boundaries unless you're in a romantic relationship with someone. That relationship puts up boundaries that a real, true friend will not cross. Your friend will respect your partner just as he or she respects you. Your friend will stay out of the business that is between you and your partner. A true friend will not encourage you to do bad things against your partner. The only time a friend should cross that boundary is if the person you're with is treating you badly. A real friend will not let you hurt yourself. Only fake friends will cross that boundary. Fake friends will try to encourage you to do wrong. Fake friends will stab you in the back. Fake friends will go to the person you're with and say things about you that aren't true. You have to be careful about which of your acquaintances you call your friends. Everyone is not your friend.

Let Go

If you can't forgive those who have hurt you, why would you expect God to forgive you? He would, because he is a forgiving God, but why would you expect it? Some people give up on life because of negative experiences. Maybe their love lives didn't go they wanted them to. Maybe someone mistreated them throughout their lives. Maybe they grew up in a bad environment where people were robbing and killing. Maybe they saw people getting shot or beat up for no reason. Or maybe they saw how so-called friends treated their so-called friends.

These people see that the world is negative, so they give up on life. Their hearts fill up with hate and negativity. They become selfish. They become envious. What they don't know is that the hate they have built up is killing them from the inside. They're letting their bad emotions take over. The sad part about it is they don't even notice.

In life, some people get scared, and the easiest thing they can do is run. Then they feel down and depressed. The more you try to run and hide from your problems, the more you think about all the problems you have. Then you start feeling bad. I have been there. I know what it feels like.

When my bad emotions get me down, I feel that I have failed in life. Sometimes I feel that I have failed as a parent. I feel that everyone in my life has let me down. I feel that no one's going to love me for who I am. I feel that I am a big mess up, no one likes me, I am a big mistake, I don't belong here, I am ugly, I am worthless. I feel like doing the world a favor and taking myself out. But—and there is a big but—when I'm feeling that way, I ask God for guidance. God always talks to us. We just have to listen. I know it sounds funny, but God talks to you in many different ways. All you have to do is listen.

Yes, I hurt. Yes, I sit up at night and cry about issues that are going on in my life. I'm not perfect, but I know one thing: I am God's child. My Heavenly Father will not let my pain, my hurt, my worries keep me down. What I am saying is this: God has your back. You just have to keep faith that he is going to deliver you out of that negative stage in your life. He will get you to your Promised Land that he has for you. Just keep breathing and doing the right thing. God will do the rest.

Live life! Don't let life run you. It is hard not to listen to the bad emotions. Giving up seems so much easier than fighting. Emotions are hard to control. Sometimes I let my bad emotions control me—what I do, what I think, and what I say to people. That's not me. I'm sorry. I'm not perfect. You just have to catch yourself and realize that you are better than that. Your emotions dictate who you are or have become. Emotions can lead you into a world of trouble, or they can lead you to your greatest accomplishments. Sometimes when you get hurt, angry, sad, or scared you start to affect others around you in a negative way.

Never let negative emotions control who you are. When you

give in to that negativity, you end up regretting what you have done to others. Bad emotions cause bad things to happen. The far extreme is people taking their own lives or the lives of others, especially if it's someone they truly love. The perpetrators do not understand that their actions are driven by their negative emotions.

You have to catch yourself when you are feeling down. You just have to weather the storm. God will not put you through anything that you cannot handle. I know it's hard to control emotions. Just hang in there. Keep breathing and surround yourself with positive experiences and people. I know the pain that comes from hurt. You don't think anyone cares, or your experiences are so bad you can't bear them. You don't think you can live. You don't think you can breathe or survive. But trust me and hold on! Everything will be all right. God is always on your side. Eventually you will find love and that happiness you have been waiting for.

Love conquers all. Love starts within yourself. Love is all you need to control your emotions in a positive way. So keep moving, keep breathing, and never give up on doing the right thing because eventually it all pays off.

There are all kinds of emotions. If you lose someone you truly love due to death or abandonment, you feel sad. When you're sad, you hurt on the inside. Then you think about that person, which leads you to over think the situation. Then you start thinking about "if only" scenarios. You blame yourself. You think everything is your fault. You fall deeper into your sadness. Sadness leads you into other emotions. When you are sad, loneliness soon follows. When you're feeling lonely, you feel a void; something is missing. You try to fill that void, and if you are rejected, you feel that no one wants you. You feel that you're ugly, everyone is against you, everyone hates you. You wish you looked like someone else. You feel nasty because no one wants to be with you.

Depression kicks in. Now you feel worthless, hopeless, and lost. You feel as if you don't know anything. You start doubting yourself. You want to be alone, shut up in a closed room. You overthink your situation even more. You wonder if anyone will miss you if you were to die. Maybe the world would be better off without you. Sadness is an emotion that can lead you to self-destruction.

When you are angry, you feel hurt, betrayed, and disrespected. You feel as if you can't believe the situation you are in. You feel that other people really tried to do you wrong. This leads to total negative thinking as well as overthinking. That's when envy comes into play. You think about ways to get back at the people you believe wronged you. You wish bad things will happen to them. The more you think about the negativity of the situation, the more negativity grows and settles in. You become even more angry. Now you're ready to fight. You are ready to destroy things. You are ready to do something physically to hurt those you now call your enemies. When you can't get to them or can't get to them the way you want to, you overthink even more.

Hate rears its ugly head. Now you're ready to destroy by any means. You are ready to get back at them anywhere or at any time you can get them. You will put yourself in jeopardy to get at them.

Is all of that worth it? Let it go. I know sometimes it's easier said than done. When I start feeling sad or angry, I try to spend time with some positive people, or I try to do something positive to keep my mind occupied on good, happy things. Keep your mind occupied on something positive. Time heals all wounds. Over time, as you heal, you will be able to let go of that sadness, that angry feeling, or that hate you have built up inside.

If you don't do this, all you are doing is stressing yourself out, and that is something you don't want to do. There is good stress, and there is bad stress. Now, you are probably reading this and wondering what I am talking about—good stress? Let me explain! You experience good stress when you have a baby or your team wins. Something that excites you for the moment. Something that is positive. Your body is made for good stress. Once the excitement is over, your body rests back to normal. Bad stress leads to bad health. The more you think about the bad situation, or the more you think negative thoughts, the more unhealthy you become mentally and physically. Bad stress sticks with you; it's hard to get rid of. You hurt, so you're constantly thinking about the situation. This sends your heart and brain into overdrive. I will come back to good stress and bad stress later.

My grandfather always told me: "Right don't wrong nobody." In other words, you always have two choices: right choice and a wrong choice. If you make the right choice, you won't be in the wrong no matter how someone else looks at the situation. For every action there's a reaction. If you do something bad, expect a bad reaction. If you do something good, expect a good reaction. If you rob a bank, you are going to jail. If you go to college and graduate, you can start a career that can lead you away from crime. Again—for every action there's a reaction.

Why would you choose do something that is against the law? When some people break the law and get arrested, they blame the police. Their choices were not the fault of the police. The police are just doing their job. Too many people in the world today are doing a lot of negative things and expecting to get something positive out of their actions. That's not how it works. When you do something negative, there will be negative consequences. When you do something positive, there will be positive rewards.

Do unto others as you would have them do unto you. Do you remember those words? Treat people with respect. Treat people the way you want to be treated. If you slap someone, don't expect them to bring you flowers. Lots of people want to blame other people when things go wrong in their lives. That is a big problem in this world! People make wrong choices and blame them on someone else so they don't feel guilty. Don't try to put things off on someone else. We have to start looking at ourselves. No one can get you in trouble but you. If you are in the car with someone, and that person jumps out and robs a bank while you're in the car, you're going to jail right along with the robber. Most people in that situation, as soon as they are arrested, want to blame everyone but themselves when they knew they should not have been in the car in the first place. Now, if you're in the car with someone who is going to rob a bank, and you get out of the car before it happens, you're not going to jail. Think about it! How many times have you done something that you know you shouldn't have done? I'm not perfect. I'm in the same boat as everyone else.

When I was in the fifth grade. I got jealous for the first time. The boy I was jealous of was popular in school. I was ignored. The teachers liked him and always gave him compliments. Our teacher felt pity for me because she knew I was poor. The principal liked him. The principal felt the same as the teachers. All the girls liked him. They thought he was cute. They didn't even know I existed. He got good grades. I didn't. His mom and dad were still together. My parents were divorced, and they were each dating other people who didn't like me. The boy and his family used to go on family vacations to lots of wonderful places. I used to have to work every day. Seeing how he was treated, I let it get to me.

One day in class, I started picking on him. He didn't want to fight back. I should have left it alone, but I didn't! I kept at him. He got angry, but he just sat there. I couldn't leave it alone. I walked over to him and leaned on his shoulder. I put all my weight on his shoulder while he was just sitting there. What I didn't know was that he bruised easily. I looked into his eyes. I saw that he was angry and scared. At that point, I left him alone, and I even apologized, but that was a little too late. When we were out at recess, somehow his shirt moved a certain way, and the teacher saw what looked like a bruise on his collar bone. She pulled his shirt back, and there it was—a big bruise. She asked what happened. He told her. She called the principal to see it. The principal took me to his office to ask me what had happened. I told him exactly what happened. He told me that I had hit the boy. I told him I hadn't, but he didn't believe me. I got suspended for three days. When I got home, I told my grandfather, and he tore my butt up. While I was suspended, my grandfather worked the heck out of me. It was as if my last name was Kinte and my first name was Kunta. The first day of work, all I thought about was getting payback. I wanted to fight the little boy. On the second day of work, I was still angry, but I felt calmer. On the third day, I was angry, but I was angry at myself. The reason I got to that point was my grandfather' philosophy. He had been talking to me every day. He told me that only I could get myself in trouble. He also told me to treat people the way I want to be treated. He told me that "right don't wrong nobody." He kept talking to me. When I got back to school. I apologized again to that little boy. He said it was okay. He told me that he told the teacher and the principal that I hadn't hit him, but they hadn't believed him, and that was why I had been suspended for three days.

I learned then that there are some things you just have to let go of. Some things just get worse before they get better. You should never let anyone push you to your limits. For some people, letting go is easy to say but not easy to do. You know your mind. You know your body. You know what it takes to get you to your boiling point. Why would you put yourself in that predicament? Before you get to that point, let it go. Move on to something positive.

A girl I once dated and I were at her friend's house. Her friend's boyfriend pulled up, got out of the car, and started walking fast over to me. He got all in my face telling me I had told his girlfriend things about him that weren't true. I was trying to tell him that I wasn't the one who had been saying those things, but he didn't want to hear anything I had to say. He pushed me. I balled my hands up, and I was going to hit him. But I was bigger, stronger, faster, and way younger than he was, and I felt that I could have seriously hurt him. At that one brief moment, I thought to myself, *I have kids. I have a good job. I have a clean record. I have goals. I have dreams. Do I really want to throw all that away over someone who is not happy with his life and risk going to jail? No I do not! I love how I am. I love my life. Why throw it away on someone who doesn't care about his life?* So I unclenched my fist and told my girlfriend to get back in the car. We got in the car and drove away.

Sometimes it's best to let go. In situations like that, you can only make it worse. Just let it go. Some people think that, if they let certain situations go, they will look weak. They will look like punks. Well think about this: how many times have you done something that messed your life up that you could have avoided? How many times have you been in a situation when you could have just let go? It's all on you. It's all about how you treat the situation.

Now I'm not saying I'm perfect! I mess up from time to time. About seven years ago. I met someone. She was very nice. She was going to school for a career. She was a year older than me. She was a good cook. She went to church regularly, and she did not go out to the clubs. She was loyal. When we started dating, I had just finished a relationship with a woman who treated me badly. I wasn't ready for another relationship, but I was lonely and was looking for companionship. I'm not trying to make excuses. What happened was all my fault; I can admit that. I should have waited before I jumped into another relationship. I treated her wrong. I wasn't around when I should have been, and I messed around with another woman. Yes, me! The other woman didn't deserve that either. I just didn't trust women. I had been treated so poorly by women over the past few years, I thought all women were that way. That's how my mind was at that time. And because of that, I should have sat back and got myself together before I thought about entering into another relationship. I should have let go of all that hurt and anger that was built up in me. Because I didn't, I hurt people who didn't deserve to be hurt. They had done nothing bad to me. Two years ago, I ran into that lady, and I had apologized. Being the woman that she is—very nice and polite—she forgave me. We still talk from time to time. I was totally wrong in that situation. I look back at my mistakes and learn from them. I don't dwell on the past. I learn from my experiences and let them go.

It's hard letting some things go—like love. Only time heals that hurt, and you will heal. When you love someone deeply, and he or she breaks up with you, it hits you hard. Some people think they can't go on living; they want to kill themselves. Some people want to hurt others. Trust me! I have been there. As much as it hurts, you have to find a way to let it go. I'm not saying jump into another relationship, because all you might end up doing is hurting the next person. Let your past relationship go before you get into another one. Let it go and stay positive!

For me, staying positive is a better way to live life. Pour some water halfway into a glass. Some people look at the glass as half empty. I look at the glass half full. In life, some people who look at the glass and see it half empty don't even know that they are doing it. They think they are doing what they have to in order to survive. Some people think they have to come across in a negative way in order for people to listen to them. They come off in a negative way in order to get things done. You don't have to come off in a negative way!

I once dated a girl for five years off and on. She did everything in a negative way. If she wanted something done, she'd yell at the person, so he or she would do it. She came across negative all the time. Everything she did was negative. When I met her, she had a seven-year-old daughter. She yelled at the little girl for everything. I used to tell her that she could attract more bees with flowers than she could with vinegar. She asked what I meant. I told her that, if she planted flowers all around, bees would come from all over to collect the pollen and nectar. Now, on the other hand, vinegar is poison to bees! I told her that it's the same with people. If you treat them with respect—treat them the way they want to be treated—they will respect you. If you treat them with disrespect, they will eventually disrespect you. I told her it was the same with her daughter. If she kept treating the child harshly, the negativity would eventually build up in her, and the child would respond by lashing out. She didn't believe me. She kept yelling at her daughter. All I could do was talk to the woman's daughter and try to show her a better way. She looked at me like a dad. I treated her as if she was my own. When she did something wrong, I talked to her about it. When she did something good, I rewarded her. Her mom and I broke up, but eventually her mom learned to humble herself and treat people with respect. She learned that being negative is not the way to go. She let all the negativities go.

Being negative is not a way of life. Let the negativity go.

Be positive. Believe in people. Most importantly, believe in yourself. Sometimes even family members come at you the wrong way. Let it go. That's family. Family members are supposed to be there when no one else is. Family members are supposed to pick you up when you're down. You should never give up on family, and family should never give up on you. Whatever disagreements you and your family members have, let them go.

A grudge is not worth holding on to. Holding a grudge is not healthy. It's not good for your body, and it's not good for your mind. A grudge is a form of bad stress. Do you remember what I said about bad stress? It is unhealthy for you. When you hold a grudge, it sends your mind into overthinking. Every time someone mentions the person's name that you are holding a grudge against, your mind starts racing. Your heart starts pumping faster. You send your body into stress mode. Again! Bad stress is not good for you. It takes a lot longer to get over bad stress than it does to get over good stress. It also takes your body a lot longer to rest itself. Bad stress can lead to chest pains, high blood pressure, heart disease, headaches, insomnia, and stomach problems. You really don't want bad stress. It is hard for your body to reset after bad stress. Be careful. Don't stress over what you can't change. There are a lot of things I wish I could change, but I can't. I just think positively, and I keep myself calm. It is hard not to think about the bad things in life. It is hard not thinking about the past, but you have to let it go in order to live your life in a positive way. The past will always be in you—the good and the bad.

My mom is a minister now, but she wasn't always the sort

of person who might be a minister. My mom has her own testimony. She has not always been a good mom even though she always loved us. No one is perfect. Not me. Not you. I love my mom with all my heart and soul. When I was a kid, I barely saw my mom.

I was hungry a lot when I was growing up. There were many days when we didn't have food to eat, but when we did get food, we got flour, ground beef, oatmeal, or rice. My grandfather would cook either big, thick pancakes that were raw in the middle; hamburgers that were not cooked all the way through; watered-down oatmeal; or gummy rice that looked like oatmeal. I loved my grandfather. He was a great man, but he could not cook! I think he was the worst cook on the planet.

One day, we did not have anything to eat. I remember that day as if it was yesterday. I made a fishing pole out of a stick, and I found some old fishing line and some old rusty hooks. I had to walk about a mile to the fishing pond. I caught five fish, and I took them home. I remembered how my dad used to clean fish, and I cleaned mine just like he did. I remembered how my mom once cooked fish that my dad had caught. I did exactly what she did. The fish came out perfect. Just as the fish was done, my mom came home. I didn't think anything of it. When she came into the house, she smelled the food and asked who was in her kitchen cooking. I said I was. I wanted her to be proud of me, but she wasn't. She whipped my butt for being in her kitchen cooking. I was so hurt—not from the whipping, but from her not acknowledging that I was really hungry. She was more worried about her kitchen being dirty. I never even got a chance to eat that fish.

My mom never was home when I was a child growing up. She wasn't there when I needed her. When I was in my late teens, she came home. A few months after my eighteenth birthday, she became sober. I was so proud. She is still doing well. She is not on drugs and never looked back at them. I am going to be honest. She and I still don't see eye to eye sometimes, but she is my mom, and I love her a lot. I went through a lot of negative experiences because of her, but I don't dwell on it. I let it go. I focus on the future, not the past. Dwelling on the past can destroy your future.

There is no grudge worth holding onto. Holding grudges can cause you to miss some of the best times you could have. My cousin had a heart attack. Before that happened, he and I were really close. When he had his heart attack, I was devastated. He got out of the hospital, and he started getting better. When I called him one day, he didn't pick up. He thought he hit the end button, but he didn't. He had hit the loudspeaker button. I overheard him and my brother saying bad things about me. Instead of calling them back later to figure it out, I just stopped talking to them at all. I was holding the biggest grudge against them. I didn't speak to them for two years.

One day, my friend's grandmother passed away. That family was bickering over who would get what from her possessions. They were not getting along at all. They just had everything negative to say about each other. They were so negative, they acted as if they didn't even care that she had died. I thought to myself, *Do I really want this to happen to me, my cousin, and brother?* I did not want that to happen to us. I called my brother and talked to him. We talked for a while. I explained why I was angry. He listened. We came to an understanding. I found out where my cousin was living at the time. I went to his house, and we talked. I explained to him why I was angry, and he listened. We came to an understanding. Now we are all close. I just didn't want to end up bickering back and forth. I didn't want to hold a grudge anymore. It wasn't worth it. I feel great now. We all get along just fine now. I had to learn to let it go.

You should never hurt someone because of the chip that's on your shoulder. Let it go. Talk it out. You never know if that person is meant to be there in the future for you. You never know who will be there when you're down. You never know who will come to your rescue when you really need them. The same person that you're holding a grudge against just might be the one who is supposed to pick you up. Or you might be the person who is supposed to pick him or her up!

My brother—the one I was holding a grudge against—was the one who pulled me out of holes on many occasions. My cousin pulled me out a few holes too. If I had still been holding a grudge, I may never have got out of those holes. I know sometimes it's hard to let go, but in the end, you will be blessed if you do. I can only say what I know, or what I have been through. Tell people what you have been through. You never know who you are helping.

Some people don't even tell others that they love them. They do love, and they show it, but they don't tell them. Has anyone told you they love you today? Have you told anyone you love them? Sometimes life will throw you a curve, and it seems that when you, your family members, and friends are going through it, most of the time, it is over something petty. Then you end up fighting and not speaking to each other. That's not what God has planned for you. God gives you free will, and it's up to you to control your emotions. I get it. We are only human, and I know sometimes it's hard to let it go. Yes, I have said this multiple times, but what happens if you never get a chance to say, "I'm sorry"? Sometimes those words are all it takes. How would you feel if God didn't forgive you? You have to think about that. Just let it go. You only hurt yourself when you hold a grudge. It's time to forgive and let go while you have time. Let's be honest—not everyone is going to see tomorrow. Love and forgive people. Remember to also love yourself. Loving yourself is very important.

Women, you are beautiful without tattoos. God has already made you beautiful. You don't need makeup, weave, fake booty, fake breasts, fake nails, face injection, bleached skin, or anything like that. Real men don't care about that stuff. They only care about you. You're perfect just the way you are. You are a queen.

Men you don't need to sag, sell drugs, be tatted up, have dreads, have gold teeth and act like you're tough or cool. Just be you. A real woman is not going to care about all those things. Be the man you are supposed to be. Love, protect, and provide.

Men and women, let go of trying to make other people happy. Make yourselves happy, and the rest will follow. Let go.

Let God

"Let him who is without sin!" Do you remember these words? Why are we judging? God didn't make certain people better than others. We are all equal. Different color, different size, man or woman—it doesn't matter! We are all equal! What right does a skinny person have to talk negatively about an overweight person? What right does a person have to think he or she is more beautiful than the next? We are not meant to be the same, and no one is perfect! We are all beautiful in our own way. How are we going to stop our kids from bullying when we do it ourselves? They learn from us. How would you like to be bullied? We need to be there for each other. We can go a long way in life if we pull together. The world would be a better place. Again! You never know who you will need. You never know who will be there to help you to get better in life.

Love thy neighbor. Remember—let's make a difference. Always be careful of what you do and how you treat people. I know I'm not perfect. I know I messed up a lot, but that's what change is all about. God will forgive you no matter what. There is no sin greater than another. A sin is a sin, but you can be forgiven. The Heavenly Father loves you. We just have to love him back. On my way to work, I thank God for everything in my life, my family members, and my friends. Everyone is a special person in his or her own way. Everyone has faults, but the Heavenly Father is there to get you through them.

Keep faith, and you can make it through anything, and I mean anything that comes your way. Don't ever give up. With faith, you will always make it through. God has blessed us with each and every day. Instead of living with bitterness, drama, regret, hate, envy, unforgiving, grudges, and depression in our hearts, we should be happy that the Heavenly Father gave us another day in which we can correct our mistakes. It's hard for some of us, but that's why we have to stick together as family members and friends. Be there for each other. Always be the best you can be. Put God first in whatever you're trying to do. It will be better than you expected. God always has his hands on you, and with God's hands, you can do anything.

When you get a blessing, help someone else shine with you. There is enough light for everybody. That light that you share will shine way brighter than before. Make God proud. God gives us free will to do whatever we want to do with our lives. That is his personal gift to you. You have the decision to do whatever you want to do. You will have wrong choices, and right choices. It's up to you to make those choices. Blessings go a lot further than luck. Blessings go for a lifetime. Luck is there for the moment.

I know sometimes it seems that, if you do bad things, good things happen, and when you do good things, bad things happen. As I said before, for every action there is a reaction. If you hold on till the end of the journey, you will see that those who make wrong choices will receive negative results, and those who make right choices will be rewarded. That's how that works. Those who make good choices just have to weather the storm until there is a break in the clouds to let the sunshine through. There will be sunny days, but until then, hold on to that umbrella. I know that I am not perfect. I have a lot to work on, but I try to do the right thing. I try to do right by people. When I pass on, I do not want God to ask me this question: "Why did you do it!" What am I going to say? What should I do? Lie to him? I'm pretty sure that's not going to work. It is so much easier just to do the right thing. You don't have to be perfect. Just be you. God will always shine down on the righteous. Live for today and do the right thing. You can never get today back.

If you have read everything in this book up to this point, you will have read in the Love chapter about the time I moved out of state with a woman. I lost everything. What I didn't tell you then was that, after that I lost everything, I talked down to God. I mocked him! At one point, I even stopped believing. Yes, me! It happens to the best of us. After that, everything I did went wrong. Nothing went right. Every time I thought I was making progress, my efforts failed. I thought I was getting ahead, but I was walking backward. I couldn't ever get it right no matter what I did.

One day, my cousin asked me to go to his house. I said I would. He lives about twenty-five to thirty miles away from me. He was already close to my house anyway. He asked me to ride with him, and I did. At the time, he was living at his mom and dad's house. They are very religious. Out of the blue, my cousin asked me to go to church with them. Well, because I was in that negative frame of mind, I tried to come up with every excuse I could. At first I said that I had something to do. That was knocked down. My cousin said that, when we got out of church, he would to help me do it. Then I said I hadn't brought any clothes suitable for church. I just knew they didn't have anything for me to wear. My waist size was quite a bit larger than theirs! I thought to myself that was a good idea. All I have to say about that is that, If God wants you, he is going to get you. My uncle went into his room and came out with a pair of pants that would fit me. I thought, *You've got to be kidding me!* I respect my uncle and aunt so much that I gave in. I got dressed. When I got in the car, there was gospel music playing. I remember the first song: "I'm Just a Nobody" by the Williams Brothers. That one song touched me in a way that I have never been touched before. The words grabbed me: "I'm just a nobody. Trying to tell everybody. About somebody. Who can save anybody."[1]

That song perfectly described who I was before I lost my faith. It's about a country boy who is trying to talk about God to everyone. The song is about someone who lost everything, but God picked him to preach the word. At church, my other uncle was the preacher. He talked about faith, the Promised Land, and never giving up. I knew it was God. I knew right then God wanted me, but he hadn't finished working on me. I went through a lot more trials and tribulations. God is still not finished with me yet. I still get my faith tested, but I hold on.

---

[1] Written by Melvin Williams, Leonard Williams, Douglas Le Allen Williams, and Stacey Todd Townsend.

God has, over the years, blessed me so much. All I'm saying is this: Never give up. Never lose faith. Your Promised Land can be right around the corner. Keep fighting. Keep breathing. Keep moving.

I am a true believer. Every time I feel as if I'm about to fall, God catches me. But God is not going to move unless you move. Some people will give up on God. I guess that's the easy thing to do. Some people don't believe in God. What if you're wrong? Are you willing to take that chance? I have seen what he can do. God is amazing. God works miracles that you wouldn't believe. I am a miracle. There are atheists who believe only in science. Well, I'm going to tell you that there are some scientists who say that some things are too complex to explain. They say the universe is so perfectly put together that scientists will never be able to figure it out. They say it had to be a higher being who built the universe. Atheists don't want to believe that because it's a lot easier to do nothing than to do something.

My family—including me—came from nothing. All we had was faith. My grandfather lived in a house that was not well put together; in fact, his house was junk. That house survived multiple hurricanes, tornadoes, and violent storms. The only thing that was holding the house together was God. Sometimes faith is all you have. Just hold on to it, and there will be a brighter day. God knows what you're going through. Some people want God to do everything. That's not how it works. God put things in place so you can make moves. Some people don't see that. They just stop having faith because they are too lazy to move for themselves. God is not going to see you sitting on the couch not trying, and send you $5,000,000, and say, "Here you go!" No! It does not work that way. God wants to see how much you want it.

Maybe you know people who are constantly getting into trouble and not trying to do what they need to do to survive. Every time you bail them out of trouble, they go right back and do the same thing and get into more trouble. How long will it be before you say "Enough!"? How long before you stop helping them? The thing is, people have to help themselves. God never stops helping you. He is just waiting on you to move. When I gave up on faith, I sat around because I didn't want to do anything. I blamed God for everything. God was doing his part. I was just too blind to see it. Once I got my faith back and started following the path he made for me, things started to get better for me. The faith I have now can't be broken.

Remember when I said that love is the most important of the five Ls? The reason is that love is in *all* the Ls. Love is in the live chapter because you have to love yourself. Love is in the love chapter because you have to show compassion for the one you're in love with. Love is in the laugh chapter because you have to love everyone, especially family members and friends. Love is in the let go chapter because you have to love being humble and caring enough to let go. Love is in the let God chapter, because God is love, and love is God. Love always starts with God.

If there is no love, there is no God. If there is no God, there is no love. People think God doesn't do anything for them. God does more than you know. You have to learn to listen when he speaks. God talks to you all the time. It might be in a song. It might be through a stranger. It might be through a person you haven't seen in a long time. It might not even be through people.

He might give you an answer by doing something amazing— like make the impossible possible. Yes, he will do it.

Several years ago, I had a terrible month of December. Everything that could have gone wrong that month went wrong. My work at that time was lawn care, so work was slow. I wasn't making much money, if any at all. If I didn't pay my electric bill, my power would be disconnected by the end of the day. We were running out of food. The kids were not going to have a Christmas. I was feeling depressed. I asked God for guidance. Then my phone started ringing. I wasn't going to pick it up, but something told me to answer. It was my brother. He was just calling to check on me. I guess he had a feeling that something might not be right. He asked me how I was doing, and I told him the situation. He told me to call my other brother and ask him for the money. I said I had just asked him the night before. He told me to just call him again as soon as we ended our call. Just as I hung up the phone, it rang again. It was my other brother. He asked how I was doing. I told him. We talk for a little while. The next thing I knew, he was at the door. He told me he had come into some money that morning, and he wanted to help me out. He gave me money for the light bill and the food. I was so thankful for that. Right after he left, my boss called to check up on me. I told him that I had a situation and that my brother had helped me out. My boss came to my house and gave me another $300 so the kids would have a Christmas. He even brought presents for them. It was so amazing that year. It turned out my boss had got some money in, and he just wanted to help me out. It was all God that day. I didn't know how I was going to pay the bills or eat, but it all happened. I didn't know where I was going to get the money. Your blessings might not come when you want them, but they will come on time.

When you're with God, it's never your time; it's always his time. All you have to do is ask, and you shall receive. Some people say they asked but they haven't received anything. It's all about patience. You want it now. God knows when you really need it. He will not give you something because you want it. He will give what you need when you need it. God has never let me down. God will never let you down. You will only let yourself down.

You will always stay down until you start walking the path that God has made for you. Some people try to walk paths that were not meant for them. Other people try to build their own paths. Then they always wonder why they run into dead ends. The path that God has for you will never lead you wrong. That path that he has for you will get longer, and wider. As long as you stay on that path, you will never have to stress because God is already working on clearing your troubles from that path.

As a teenager, I grew up hard. As I have mentioned, we were very poor. When I was eighteen, I got tired of not eating and not having nice things. I decided that I was going to become a street boy. I was going to sell drugs to make money and buy all the things I wanted. There is a saying: more money, more problems. That is not a lie. Yes, I was eating. Yes, I had new things. But I also started accumulating a whole lot of so-called friends. Everything seemed good, but it wasn't. I had to constantly look over my shoulder to watch for others. I was always trying to hide from the police. Every time I made enough money to quit selling drugs, it seemed I always had to spend that money I had made on something else. It never failed. Every time I saved, I had to spend. I tried everything to save money, but it wasn't working. I had bought myself a car. I thought I was doing good. Wrong!

One day, I was driving down the road, and the police pulled me over. They asked me where the guns and drugs were. I denied everything. They told me to get out of the car. They made me get on the ground. They start searching my car. I just knew I was going to go to jail because there were drugs in the car. They searched for about an hour. They didn't find anything. They let me go. They never looked in the ashtray. That's where the drugs were. The ashtray was open the entire time. I don't know how they didn't see it. Needless to say, that was my last day of selling drugs. God had my back that day. I will never forget what God has done for me.

God made me into who I am today. God doesn't owe us anything. He gives because he loves us. It's like when you have kids. You don't owe them anything, but you constantly give them everything—not because you owe them, but because you love them. You want them to have the best. You want them to be the best. That's just because you love them. That's why God loves us. God wants us to be the best. He wants us to succeed. Problems are going to come and go. You have to believe that God will handle those problems for you. Give your problems to God. God can always handle them better than you can. God has been handling my problems for years now. If you are going to pray about it, why worry about it? We are human. Yes, we are going to worry. It's in our nature, but when you give your troubles to God, you need to have faith. You won't worry as much because you know everything will work out for the best.

Everything is better left in God's hands. When you leave your life in God's hands, everything works out better than you expected. If he closes one door, you wonder why God did that. You might think that God is not working in your favor. All along, he is making everything better. He will open another door—or a window! You might lose a job, but a week later, you will have another one that is way better. Some people feel as if they are always down, and they are always broke. They can never find a good job. It's because they have lost faith, and they are not meeting God halfway. Always keep the faith. Faith is what keeps me going. There are a lot of people who say they have faith—but they don't.

This world is so corrupted with a lot of negativity. We need to learn to work together, and let God do his part. As humans, we are not getting anywhere with this hate that is everywhere. It's on television, in our schools, in our streets, in our churches, at our doorsteps.

Now what I'm going to say next might make some people angry, but it needs to be said. This is for African Americans. I often read on social media and hear people saying that the government mistreats black people, black people are always being held down, the president doesn't do anything for black people, white men enslave our people. I've even heard someone say that God is doing black people wrong. The bottom line is this: People come up with a whole lot of excuses.

Yes, blacks do have it harder, but it is all up to you to be successful. Yes, black men have to do more to succeed. It's easy to blame the next person, but if you don't try to do something, that's on you.

I hear and read everything people have to say. People talk, but how many times have you gone to the projects to mentor kids to teach them how to get out of there? How many black communities did you go to and try to hold a job fair? How many times have you seen a post on social media or heard people say they need jobs, and you tried to help them? How many times have you volunteered to help at a homeless shelter or a women's shelter? How many times have you talked to the young community about going to college? If you have done any of these things, how many times have you done them?

People talk about being black, but what have they done to help the black community? It seems to me that people do a lot of talking but those people who talk the loudest don't do anything. Talk is cheap.

Do you think the president, the local government, or God is supposed to hand you a bag full of money, a house, a car, and say go live your life? That's not how it works. You have to put in the effort. There are people in the black community who are not trying. They will do a lot of talking, but they won't try.

I'm saying this again! There are people who are making their felony record an excuse. They just do not believe in themselves. They do not believe in God and what he can do. All you have to do is let God do what he does. A friend of mine did fifteen years in prison. He got out of prison and went to school. Now he is making plenty of money welding. My family was dirt poor; we had no food, no running water, but we made it. We didn't complain about the white man keeping us down. We did what we had to do to make it.

I love being black, and I would do anything to help my black community, but what I won't do is talk without taking action. I just *do*. People are talking, but I don't hear anything. Your success is on you. Not the government. Not God. It's on you. Black business owners, start talking to that young brother in the streets who needs a job. As members of the black community, we need to start telling the young girls it's not cool to have sex and act all grown up. Tell them that they don't need all that fake booty and breasts. Teach them to love the skin they are in. Let's teach our brothers and sisters to stop the violence. Let's teach our people how to be better people for our kids.

The black community is angry, outraged, and protesting because the good cops won't stand up to the bad cops. They won't do anything. They won't say something to other cops for shooting and killing black people. If it makes you angry that cops are killing black people, then why aren't the good people in the communities standing up, doing anything or saying something when our own people are killing each other? Where is the protest? Where is the outrage? So you are saying it's okay if we kill ourselves, but it's not okay for police officers to kill us. Shouldn't black lives matter no matter who is doing the killing? Don't half do something. If you are going to do it, do it all the way. If black lives matter to you, live that belief 24/7, not only when you want it to matter.

Yes, black lives do matter. As good people, we should stand up against killing no matter who is doing the killing or who is getting killed. Our community should stand up and come together to work toward a better future. For the past month, I have seen reports on the news and social media about people who have been shot or stabbed. Just killed for no reason. People ooh and ahh for a day or two on social media, but that's it.

Where are the good people in the community? They are not standing up and doing something about the violence. Why? It wasn't police officers who killed them? Lives should matter no matter who is killing people. As of right now, the government is doing the same thing so many citizens are doing—doing a lot of talking, but not taking action to solve the problem. If all people do is talk, their minds are still enslaved. We break the chains by doing better, not just talking. Let me say this: Where I live, there were at least eight murders last month. Now what did our community do? Nothing! All I am saying is, we need to stand up no matter if the police kill someone or other blacks do it. We as a community need to rise up as one strong unit. We are doing a lot of talking, but what are we actually doing? I'm not saying blacks kill blacks at a higher rate than other races kill their own. I'm saying it all needs to stop. If we wait for the government to act, things will never get better, but if we stand up as one unit, we can accomplish anything. We can be successful. It's all on us.

Men of color, we have to stop degrading our women. Stop calling women out their names. We need to embrace our women and treat them with respect. Stop trying to do things you see on television or hear on the radio. Just be you. You don't need to impress someone who is not important to you. Impress God. Impress your kids if you have any. Impress your wife. Don't try to impress people on the streets. Those people not important enough to impress. Young boys are watching everything we do. They watch how their elders talk to and treat women. They watch how their elders run their houses and interact with individuals and the community. They watch their elders' work ethics. They watch every move their elders make. If they grow up and end up in and out of jail or doing the wrong things because their elders have set the wrong example, how can we get mad at them? Those boys were just doing what they were taught. If we want them to do better, we have to teach them better. We are not doing our jobs as men. They didn't let us down. We let them down. We need to be better role models. We need to raise our boys to be men. Not thugs. Not dope boys. Not niggas. None of that. Just raise them to be responsible, respectable, loyal, loving men. Let's do the right thing. You are the only ones who are stopping you from being successful. You are the only ones who can get yourselves in trouble. God sees all.

Women of color, you have to stop putting black men down. When they start dating outside their race, you put them down even more. Did you ever stop to think maybe you need to lift black men up? Stand with your man. Stop always trying to run after things that are not good for you. Like no good men! Stop disrespecting yourself. Show some self-respect. If you want men to respect your mind, you have to start respecting your mind yourself. Stop letting men degrade you and define who you are. Every time you do something, little girls are watching you. They look at the pictures you put on social media. They watch how you dance. They watch how you treat men. They watch your every move. If she has sex at an early age, or posts a video of herself twerking half naked on social media, and you have set a bad example, how are you going to get angry? You can't get mad at her. That little girl is just doing what she was taught. You need to raise your little girls to be ladies. Not bad bitches. Not trap queens. Not hoes. Just raise them to be responsible, respectable, loyal, loving ladies. Do the right thing. You're the only one that can stop you from being successful. You're the only ones who can get yourselves in trouble. God sees all.

Black men and women, you are great, but until we realize it, we are still going to be sitting around doing nothing but complaining. Stand up and start doing! We need to stop putting down our own race and start lifting ourselves up to be great. God sees all.

Caucasian men! Stop downgrading women. Stop thinking women can't do anything. My boss is a woman, and she does a great job. Stop putting down every race. Stop looking at a person's skin. Look into a person's heart. People are more than just skin. White men, stop putting down your own race. Just because other people dress differently or listen to different music, that doesn't mean they are bad people. Little boys are watching your every move. If they go out and do hate crimes and end up in jail, how are you going to get angry? They are just doing what they are taught. They see how you treat women. They see how you interact with different races. They see how you interact with people of your own race. They look at everything you do. Stop teaching them to hate what they don't understand. Stop teaching them that everyone is not equal. Just raise them to be responsible, respectable, loyal, loving men. Do the right thing. You're the only one that can stop you from being successful. You're the only ones who can get yourselves into trouble. God sees all.

Caucasian women, stop letting men treat you badly. Stop thinking that the only way you can make it in life is to kiss men's butts. You have to know you are great. Stop letting men lead you into a life of hate. Stop believing that we are all not equal. Little girls are watching you every move. If she grows up letting men treat her poorly or has been led to hate and do wrong, how are you going to get angry? Those little girls are only doing what they have been taught. Do the right thing. Raise your little girls to be responsible, respectable, loyal, loving women. You're the only ones who can stop you from being successful. You're the only ones who can get yourselves into trouble. God sees all.

White men and women you are great people. We can work together as a team. We are all equal. No one is better than anybody. God sees all.

Hispanics and Latinos, you are a hard-working race. You can do anything you put your minds to. Stop settling for less. You are great. It's the same with Asians, Arabians, Italians, Samoans, and every other race on our planet. You are all great. Be who you are. Raise your kids to make the right choices. Raise them with love in their hearts. You don't have to be like someone else. You are great just the way you are. God did not make any mistakes with any of us. When the world stops seeing color and starts seeing people for who they are, we will be a better human race. God put you here to love, not hate.

How can you hate a person's skin? You don't know the person underneath that skin. There are all kinds of religions. Everyone has his or her own beliefs. There is nothing wrong with that. You have free will to believe what you want, and no one can take that away. No matter what religion you are, if you believe in your heart that your religion is the right religion for you, then you are not wrong. That is what's in your heart. All God-based religions speak of love because, no matter what your religion is, your God is love. We need more love in this world, so when I say God is love, I am speaking to all religions. When I say let God, I am speaking to all religions. Let's be better people. Let's be better humans. Let's do what we have to so we can fill the world with love, trust, good morals, and honor.

God cannot do what he does unless we let him. We need to let God. Most of us are fighting against his blessings, and we don't even know it. We think we are doing the right thing, but the thing we are trying to do is not what God wants us to do. That is not for us. That is not our blessing. We need to recognize our blessings. That person, that thing, that job, or whatever is holding you back because you think it is good for you. Let go and let God. Your blessing is only a reach away. When you let go of that negativity and let God take over, you will be better off.

Has someone ever done you wrong, and you tried to get back at him or her, but it never went right? The more you try to get back at someone, the worse the situation becomes. The moment you leave it alone and give the situation to God, the situation works out for the best. Everything gets better when you let God rather than trying to take care of the situation yourself. I get it. Instincts kick in, and you want to get back at that person. You want to cause him or her the same hurt you felt. The best thing you can do is forgive, let go, and let God. That's the only way it will work out for the best. The best way to block or beat negativity is to face it with positivity.

I was once with a woman with whom I was truly in love. She cheated on me and ended up leaving me for another man. I was devastated. I wanted to get back at her so badly. I spread rumors about her. I harassed the guy she was with. Everything I did backfired. I was so hurt that I wanted to make her hurt. The more negative I got, the happier she got. I just gave up. I just let go and let God have it. I just gave my hurt, my anger, and my pain to God. Now I have no hurt, I have no anger, and I have no pain. Sadly, her new man is treating her the same way she treated me, and I feel sympathy for her.

I don't look back at my past because I want to go back. I look at my past to learn what not to do in my future. I learn from my mistakes. I learned that negative on negative makes everything worse, but if you fight negative with positive, you get a better result. God is in everything I do. I live in faith. Faith is what keeps me motivated. Faith keeps me breathing. Faith is why I believe that this world can be a better place even with all the negativity that's in it now. We are not perfect, but we are great. Let God do it for us.

CHAPTER 6

One Last Look
at the Five Ls

There are many ways to look at this book. I just hope you look at it as a positive lesson. Life is not going to hand you everything you ever wanted. You have to get out there and make your dreams happen for yourself. One thing I've learned is to stay positive and not put anything negative into my life. I've never gotten anything out of negativity in my life. God gives us all free will. It's up to you to be successful, or it's up to you to sit back and not do anything. Yes, it's your God-given right to do nothing, but don't expect to become a millionaire and achieve everything you ever wanted. You put in nothing, you get nothing.

Taking the long path through life is hard, but you will reach your goal. Sometimes things will be easy; sometimes things will be difficult. But the most important thing is to keep moving, stay positive, and don't let anyone or anything stop you. Invest in yourself. Be in control of yourself. Never give up on yourself.

I'm going to *live* my life to the fullest. I'm going to *love* from my heart and from my soul. I'm going to *laugh*, smile, and be happy, so I will fill my soul with joy and spread happiness to others. I'm going to *let go* of anger, hate, envy, and the negativity that comes my way because all it does is break me down. It breaks down my mind, body, and soul. I'm going to *let God* handle all of my battles. He is the way. God can deal with my problems better than I can. God will not let me down.

If we handle our problems with negativity, we are going to get negative things back. If we handle our problems with positivity, will get positive things back. For every action, there is a reaction. It's up to you how you handle your problems.

Live your life. Do you really want to keep living in a world of negativity? I don't! If good people stand up and have faith, we can accomplish anything. Be the person that you know you can be. You are great. You are awesome, but you have to believe in yourself. I can't do it for you. I can only live my life and do the things I can do. You have to live yours. You're only as good as your mind says you are. If you think you're great, then you are great. If you think you're not that good, then you're not that good. You're the only one who controls your thoughts and behavior and your life. You are in control. You just have to believe and have faith. I didn't think I could write a book, but I believed that I could.

I'm not saying that, if you follow the advice in this book, you will be an overnight success. What I am saying is that you have to work at it, but you have to start somewhere. It all starts with you wanting to change. I want to be a better person for myself, my family, and my community. Aim to keep positivity in your life. As I said before, none of us is perfect. We are going to mess up from time to time. We are going to make bad decisions every now and then. Don't let that discourage you from being who you are. You just have to pick yourself up and try again. I learned that being positive makes a world of a difference for the better.

I can't tell you how to live a better life. I can only show you a path to a better life. That's your path. Only you can take that route. It's up to you to go for it. The path might not be perfect. There may be bumps in the road, but it's all about how you react to them. You have to live your life. Your friends can't do it for you. Your family members can't do it for you. The government can't do it for you. God can't do it for you. You have to do it for you. I laid out a path for you to follow. It is the path to a better you. Just follow the path of the 5 Ls:

1. **Live.** When you live, you have to love yourself. You can't love others unless you love yourself. It all starts with you. It all starts with how you feel. You are in charge of you. Self-love is very important. There is a difference in self-love and being selfish. Self-love is when you love yourself so you can love others. Selfish is when you love yourself, and only love you. Make sure it's self-love, and not selfishness.

2. **Love.** Once you have learned to love yourself, you can start loving others. You can live your life around other people without having animosity toward anyone. If you have hate and anger in your heart from your previous encounters, there will be no room for love. Love has to be pure. It's not something you can buy. Love is real. It's the best feeling you can ever have if it's true love. There is a whole lot of fake love in this world, but you will feel true love in your heart and soul. Love is never supposed to hurt. If it hurts, it's not love.

3. **Laugh.** When you have learned to love yourself and to love others, it's time to enjoy life. Laughter fills you with happiness. It fills your heart and soul with happiness. It is very healthy for you. I truly believe that laughter keeps us young at heart. It helps push all that negativity to the side. Laughter is what we all need. Laughter is the positive side of life.

4. **Let go.** When you have learned to love yourself and to love others, and you have the joy of laughter in your heart and soul, you must learn not to hold grudges. You have to let go of all that hate, all that anger, and all that negativity. Let it go. It's not worth holding on to. It is very unhealthy for you. It breaks down your body and mind. It's not good for the soul. Holding hate in is unhealthy. Just let it go. Your health and your life will improve.

5. **Let God.** Let God have your negativity. God always turns your negativity into positivity. God will never let you down. The blessings might not come when you want them, but they will come at the right time. God gives you free will, so it's up to you how you live your life. You have the chance to make wrong and right choices. If you go down the wrong path, and you end up in a place you don't want to be, it's not God's fault. It's yours! You had a chance to do the right thing, but you chose otherwise.

I will say this again—you're the only one who can get yourself into trouble. You're the only one who can stop your success. Be safe. Stay positive. Stay motivated. Do your best. Do what you feel is best for you. We are not perfect, but the good thing is that we don't have to be. We just need to be ourselves. All we have to do is be the best we can be. Encourage others to do better. Teach children the right way. Let's do what we have to do to block out the negativity. Forgive others, and let your soul be at peace. Don't hold grudges. Own up to your faults. It's okay to be wrong. We are not going to always get it right, but it's okay.

Let's embrace the love that is given to us and let go of all the hate and anger that is thrown at us. Embrace the happiness and stop the bitterness. You are the best. You are great. You are awesome. Don't expect anything less in your life. Believe in yourself. Nothing can stop you from achieving but you. Do good things. Nothing is given to you, so go out and get it. Let's move forward and do what we have to do to give our kids a better future. There is no greater feeling than appreciating and joining in a child's laughter. Let's stay on the right path. It might get bumpy sometimes, but we have to keep going, and never stop. Eventually the path will smooth out. Don't let anything stop you. The most important thing is to always keep God above it all. Through him, anything is possible. Luck goes only so far, but a blessing lasts forever.

Always remember the Five Ls:

1. Live
2. Love
3. Laugh
4. Let go
5. Let God

I love you all. Thanks for reading.

Printed in the United States
by Baker & Taylor Publisher Services